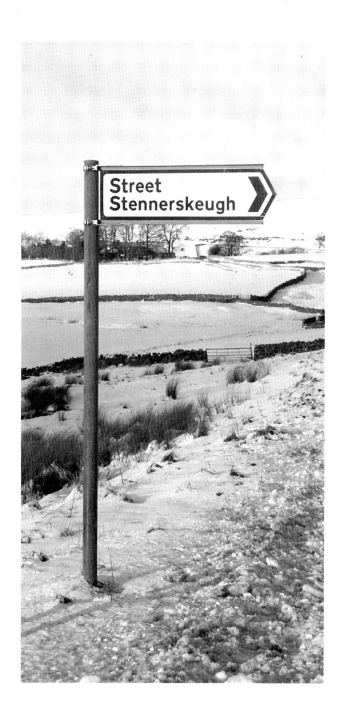

Corners around the Howgills

Gareth Hayes

HAYLOFT

First published 2004

Hayloft Publishing Ltd, Kirkby Stephen,
Cumbria, CA17 4DJ

tel: (017683) 42300
fax. (017683) 41568
e-mail: books@hayloft.org.uk
web: www.hayloft.org.uk

ISBN 1 904524 18 4

A catalogue record for this book is available
from the British Library

Produced in Great Britain
Printed and bound in Hungary

Photographs by the author except N Thexton (page 93)
and GE Hayes (page 96).
Jacket illustration by Rosemary Morison

In memory of my father,
George Edgar Hayes
(17.05.26-29.07.98)

You can only keep what you are prepared to give away.

This is a very busy world which sets hard tasks and rigid limitations for most of us. We are dimly conscious that there are precious words, throbbing with the life and experiences of earlier men, buried away in heavy, dusty books, lost to us, because we cannot spare the time to search them out. We catch a hint of these living passages as we catch the odour of flowers by the roadside; but the compulsion of business drives us on. The person who gathers them and puts them within reach of our hand does us a service. It is with this thought in mind that I have picked and bound up these passages, still fragrant with the odour of saintly lives. The busy man or woman can here, in odd moments, get a real breath of ampler ether and diviner air, unsuspected by those who see only the great forbidding books which give little suggestion of redolent perfume.   Rufus M. Jones, *Little Book of Selections from the Children of Light*, 1909

CONTENTS

ILLUSTRATIONS

Acknowledgments

It is with no doubt a feature of our character that everyone I have talked to along the path of research for this book has been helpful beyond the call. I have renewed contact with family, deepened relationships with friends and met some unique people en route. They know who they are and I am very grateful for their support, loyalty and genuine humility. I must make special thanks to the ladies of Cumbria Photo, Penrith who have not only helped me with the pictures but who have always made me smile even on my grumpiest of days.

INSPIRATION

A beautiful woman achieves immortality by the memory of the photographs that are taken of her. Those photographs can often tell a simple biography of the woman. The same portfolio of history can be taken from the canvas of countryside caught by the patient cameraman with a bent for a still life landscape. While there is clearly much more to the beautiful woman, and she will undoubtedly be different from the assumptions made through her screen persona, there is also much more to be told about the life behind the photographs of textured trees, rushing rivers, mosaic mountains. Each fell and dale, each rock and stone, each beck and pool, each home and hospitality hold many a tale.

I am lucky enough to be able to tell a few and these come from a variety of close sources. My own experiences, coloured by time and enthusiastic fondness for keen memories, are the only ones I can contend to display with complete accuracy. Family and friends relate personal experiences which themselves divert from pastel shades to a vibrant wash, and touch the hearts and amuse the souls while shimmering across the lines of truth and dream. Older tales come from books whose authors left these shores long ago and such stories may be closer to myth than gospel, yet their authority over time alights a spirit, a security, a strength in our past that ignites a faith in our being.

Edmund Bogg and Rev. W. Nichols wrote great travelogue pieces around the turn of the last century and these truly stir the imagination with wonder as we reflect rationed days of hard work and little play. Pictures coloured by words. Text to the memories. Jessica Lofthouse, Marie Hartley, Arthur Raistrick and W R Mitchell bring us within living memory, yet their tales are now very much in the past as pace and passion for countryside pales by our failing global temperament.

Tourism makes me uneasy and today's tourists more so, even though at the heart of it I am one myself, and quite a good one too. A recent Sunday visit to Keswick made me shudder at the hoards milling with aimless direction. Tourists come in all shapes and sizes. On that day I saw little variety. I do not particularly crave solitude, it just depresses me that these people cannot rise higher than their lowly plateau and spark with some creativity and courage. If they did, my own personal places and spaces would be invaded so perhaps I should be grateful. Invaded or shared? Why do I want to share my corners when I want to, need to, keep them protected?

Well, no matter how much is put in front of the noses of the Keswick crowds to lure them to different pastures they will still stick to where they believe their grass is green. Because their neighbour also believes the grass is green. Sheep. Slavishly imitating rather than daring to be different. That harsh principle aside there is a spiritual ethic in only being able to keep what one is prepared to give away.

Our tourists get off the bus, they buy a souvenir card, piece of elaborate pottery, or a 'fancy good' with Lake District inscribed and get back on the bus. The car owner queues for the car parking space closest to the shops not noticing the empty spaces beneath the fells. For me, it is like discussing the merits of a multiple-choice questionnaire against a dignified essay. If that bus took them along the Fair Mile through the Lune Gorge and dropped them off for twenty minutes to simply breathe the air and capture the texture of God's country they might tire easily and mutter boredom and long for television and tabloid. Yet, to turn one face to the fells and the spirit within would make this voice worthwhile. The souvenir, the hopeless present is simply a cry of inner loneliness and a desire to be liked. 'Look where I am and please like me.'

I am heading down a dangerous philosophical route as people have many justified and virtuous reasons for such inclinations. Small families, old families, learners, teachers. I am being far too critical and I should, and will, focus on the positive. My own material souvenir is the old postcard and a close photograph from my own camera. Indeed, I am a total fan of the postcard and collect and despatch in equal high frequency. I admit then, that there is a due parallel with my postcard affinity and my neighbour's fondness for the ferocious thimble hunt. There are very few postcards of the Howgills, just as there are very few thimbles. I hope this book will give you a fair

selection of postcards and with that, a fingerprint of identity to what the Howgills mean to me.

I like the Howgills. It may be no coincidence that they usually sit behind the Lakes, Pennines and Dales in terms of popularity and my fondness derives from that lesser distinction. Perhaps I prefer to champion the underdog as the same characteristic has me listening for music lying outside the Top Ten and eye for a the girl at the back in Miss World. I am also a Sunderland supporter. In these, I am neither alone nor unique.

We will discuss non-conformity and dissension later. For now, let us consider what picture I want to see on my postcard. And yours. There are many camera clubs and photography professionals who wax lyrical about f values, auxiliary gradients and dimensional layers. For me it is the vision in front of the camera matched by the eye behind it that matters. The cheapest of instamatics can still produce a great photograph. The mixture of composition, opportunity and attitude combined with luck, with light, mosaics of movement and corners of still-life are all to be held in frame by the observant eye. Over fragrant observance can be fraudulent and soon faced with unfashionable focus. Witness Colin Baxter. Take the picture for what you see and for what it is and rewards will come.

The Lakes, Dales and Pennines are prime fodder for film and are recognised across the globe. Encircling the Howgill Fells these three larger ranges seem to hide, or even protect, our subject from such promotional recognition. I like this.

Yet we must not think that they are a poorer relative. Indeed, closer inspection has dictated a keener focus and the Howgills have never really been ignored. And what extra pleasure is there to be found in looking a little deeper than the surface publicity. William Wordsworth called them "Naked Heights" and Alfred Wainwright famously referred to them as his "Sleeping Elephants". Gorgeous descriptions, which I cannot better.

However, I do want to examine a broader canvas, a bigger picture, and give an explanation to why this is such a special place. With cerulean skies, the comfort is almost unmanageable and reminds me of the unencumbered freedom of childhood only paralleled by the best days at the seaside.

Pride and nostalgia will drive many. A simple 'this is home' will satisfy most. That spirit of home is defined by the special race that could have, and in some case did, take the world by storm. Famous sons are many although their humility in modern times dictates little fame. In retrospect and with due consideration the impact of Howgill children is outstanding.

I would like to think that there is something in this book for everyone: from those who belong to those that don't; from hydrographers to uranographers; from geologists to ichthyologists; from train spotters to heavy rockers; from pluralists to exclusivists; from egotists to the humble; from women to men and back again; from dissenters to descendants; and, of course, to tourists.

Throughout this book the reader will discover that many of our instincts and moderations on life are accepted now because of the inspirational thoughts of the wandering shepherd with a mind for more. These people may not be in a rush for modernism, yet they practically invented it. Today, as expanding technologies, eastern spirituality and empirical philosophies redefine scientific and religious need, we can reflect on their clouded relationship through the lessons given by those Howgill children.

My own interests fall in the crossover area where the most natural of sciences, philosophy and history and applied biology, marry seamlessly yet retain their own space. Indeed, it was not until Lancaster born William Whewell coined the phrase 'scientist' in 1833 did science as a distinct discipline begin to run side by side with religion as man's inquisitive side explored age-old questions. There will be many examples in these pages of local wisdom that I will have omitted, for reasons of space and no doubt, ignorance, and I trust I can be forgiven for that. Education is a strange beast and I am still learning how best to tame it. Thankfully the hunger continues and is made more mindful by following in the steps of the Howgill Shepherd with time to observe, think and share.

William Whewell embodied the apportion of collaboration and common bond that we will see often amongst the Howgillians. After all, isn't that the core principal of education and the best way to bring up our children and have them aspire to greater things where the principles are progress not necessarily perfection? Whewell's fondness for language saw him give the words "anode," "cathode," and "ion" to iconic chemist and physicist Michael Faraday, himself of parents who belonged to the Kirkby Stephen district. This magnetic attraction to the wisdom and wonder of peripheral personalities should stop now as we set off to explore the corners that they used for their inspiration. With Faraday in mind, what better place to start than with Kirkby Stephen home to some uneasy educational experiences, some of the best fashionable peculiarities, and delightful odd corners.

Main Street, Kirkby Stephen

This education has for its first and last step humility. It can commence only because of a conviction of deficiency; and if we are not disheartened under the growing revelations which it will make, that conviction will become stronger unto the end. But the humility will be founded, not on comparison of ourselves with the imperfect standards around us, but on the increase of that internal knowledge which can alone make us aware of our internal wants. Let us consider, for a little while how wonderfully we stand upon this world. Here it is that we are born, bred, and live, and yet we view these things with an almost entire absence of wonder to ourselves respecting the way in which all of this happens. So small, indeed, is our wonder, that we are never taken by surprise... Hence we come into this world, we live, and depart from it, without our thoughts being called specifically to consider how all this takes place; and were it not for the exertions of some few inquiring minds, who have looked into these things and ascertained the very beautiful laws and conditions by which we do live and stand upon the earth, we should scarcely be aware that there was anything wonderful about it.

Michael Faraday

KIRKBY STEPHEN

Kirkby Stephen is the first significant Kirkby on our travels, the second being Lonsdale, and has not always been popular with your author. As a teenager I was wary of the place. Apart from the low gene taking me from royalist Appleby to republican Kirkby Stephen, this was misdirected sentimentality prompted by school egos and the need for my own, Appleby Grammar, school to compete with a sister Grammar at Kirkby. Of course they were not true Grammar schools having turned comprehensive some years earlier. They did share some 'Grammar' traditions like rugby and a high loyalty ethic.

We were also jealous of Kirkby Grammar because it had a swimming pool. I take no pleasure in learning of the closure of the Grammar's pool in 2003 because of safety and, inevitably, financial constrictions. This may only be slight ebb in the wrong direction as a steering group, prompted by a tide of support, is making waves to reverse the decision and hopes to launch a refreshed pool in 2004. I do hope so. I expect that sensitivity between the two schools of Kirkby Stephen Grammar and Appleby Grammar has also vanished from the curriculum as much as my returned favour for both towns.

Kirkby Stephen from Church Tower

The Church of St. Stephen dominates the centre of the town. Dating from the 13th century its commanding tower was an addition in the 16th century. Norse legend was christianised when the famous 8th century 'Loki stone' was brought into church; it is meant to depict the Devil in chains and is the only such stone to have survived in Britain, and one of only two in Europe. As such it is actually one of the few physical survivals from the time when the Vikings settled in parts of this area. The connection with the Devil is misrepresented as the

Robert Borrowdale with Barrow, Kirkby Stephen.   From Photo, G. Bell, Kirkby Stephen, 1896.

chained figure depicts the Norse God Loki, who plays a significant role in Scandinavian mythology. Most memorably for his relationship with Freyia and Frigg through persuasive cunning and then by causing the death of Odin's son, for which he was imprisoned in a stone cell and tied by chains. Do not be put off by the size of Loki when you peek inside the church. This only confirms his devilish manner.

Loki is portrayed, at the surface, to be a malevolent and evil demon, hence the confusion with things devilish. His character traits and habits give good cause to assume trickery. He has no difficulty changing his shape (appearing as a falcon, as a salmon, and as a mare) and he transgresses boundaries not only as shape-shifter but also as a manipulator of gender boundaries, being able to change his sex at will. These, I must add, are not traits I directly associate with the people of Kirkby Stephen. In Loki's defence, modern

14

have always been important as it sits on the edge of Cumbria (Westmorland) and Yorkshire; and before that always on the edge of Scottish invasion.

Local conflict is still occasionally prompted by memories of republican forces against royalist Appleby; of a curious relationship with Brough who decided they didn't want a railway and by some default let it prosper at Kirkby Stephen; and now the modern day controversy of the free parking scheme whereas the rest of Eden suffers from the wrath of the Traffic Warden Gods.

thought believes that Loki cannot always act of his own volition, but that he is often forced to act according to the desires of others.

Loki's character has been summarised as the instigator of conflict yet also as the provider. As the instigator of conflict, it was out of necessity. As the provider, he provides the most prominent establishment with precious and useful gifts, each according to the function they have.

Kirkby Stephen may be a wonderful place but there is no doubt that it transgresses the borders of Eden Valley, Howgill Fells and Yorkshire Dales. Its remoteness is both a weakness and strength. It suffers in Eden by being the furthest town away from local government at higher Carlisle and lower Penrith. Its boundaries

As provider, Kirkby delights to satisfy the needs of hungry travellers with numerous cafes, tea rooms and fish and chip shops. Kirkby is the main half-way halt for touring Geordies on their

15

way to Blackpool. If it were not for this tourism I doubt if Kirkby people would want or need such a propensity of chip shops. It has also built a reputation as an 'antique' town and such shops abound.

Were the locals of a thousand years ago so wise to recognise the symbolism of Loki? A coincidence perhaps, although they do say that a coincidence is God working in anonymity. From pagan roots and Christian evolutions the Loki Stone has probably been more associated with a reminder that the Devil, in whatever form of temptation, is to be feared and we can all stray if we don't keep him tied down.

Market Place, Kirkby Stephen

From Kirkby central the walker staying to the road heads north or south in a manner created by the traffic-busy High Street, yet greater adventures can be found to the east and west. Kirkby Stephen's alley and passageways are great fun and every time I visit I seem to discover one that was hidden the time before. Parallel to the high street is the back road named after Michael Faraday, that bright spark brought up in nearby Mallerstang; this nomenclature is a modern refinement, having previously gone by the titular Back Lane. At the lower junction with Christian Head (what a marvellous name for a street) the road turns out of Kirkby Stephen towards Soulby. High on the rising hill is Stobars Hall, built in 1829, now a residential care home

for the elderly. There cannot be many places so grand in the countryside within which to end your days.

Around here is a stile bearing off as if to circumnavigate the larger boundary of Kirkby Stephen. It may be morbid for to me make this comment but death is close by. Signposted Bloody Bones Lane, historic devilish acts of undisciplined times come to mind and the walker treads softly so as not disturb the ghosts that lie beneath. The name originates not from scandal but from tragedy. Tales vary from the town's horses being buried here after falling victim to an outbreak of a plague to a more definitive report of

a stock slaughter because of a foot and mouth outbreak in 1780. From time to time, at dusk with a new moon, wailing shrieks echo silently around the ancient hedgerows.

Less chilling, a favourite spot for many is behind the main street to the east and the beautiful River Eden. Through more tight lanes the outlook brightens and opens onto wide parkland showing the cricket pitch to one side and Gramsceugh to the other and a pleasant walk to Hartley. On the banks of the Eden there is opportunity just to sit and watch the ducks, skim stones or play Pooh Sticks from Frank's Bridge. A stone footbridge, Frank's Bridge would have been used

KIRKBY STEPHEN FROM GRAMSCEUGH

our nation offers the outstanding back drop of Roman Fell in one direction and Wild Boar Fell in the other?

Kirkby Stephen has an active community and understands the frailties of tourism. As such it occasionally attempts to re-invent itself. At the Millennium, an avenue of lime tress was planted behind the cricket fields by one of the paths that lead to Hartley and Winton via Coffin Bridge. This shows superb wisdom in looking after the next generation and the avenue will be magnificent in splendour when mature.

for narrow carts and working horses in years gone by. Today it opts for a less stressful tourist life. Why Frank? I have asked a number of local souls and have been told that the bridge has also been prefixed with Brewery and Rowlandson, yet as yet I have no clue as to the identity of Frank.

The riverbank is host to seats donated to the memory of loyal local folk and sharp-eyed observers will also be interested to see an ancient horse measuring flag set in the grass. Above the riverbank is the cricket field and a mighty splendid common it is, set in a natural arena, it fulfils the air and grace befitting cricket and all things English. A perfect place for a picnic, not on the field itself you understand, and a change of pace synonymous with our splendid game. What other cricket field in

Residents have recently announced that they intend to launch a Swaledale Sheep visitor centre at the town's auction mart. The centre would host a café and viewing area to allow the public to see

KIRKBY STEPHEN PARISH COUNCIL
STENKRITH PARK
FOOTPATH TO NATEBY Rd.

a livestock market in action. Recognising that tourism is a trade that must sit within, rather than outside, the farming community is a wise move in our new century of diversification. The idea to offer a fly-on-the-wall view of rural life is not so different than the menagerie of themes seen on today's television. The zoo has simply opened its gates and spun the camera around. The scheme has not been welcomed in all quarters. The sheep fanciers of Hawes have laid claims to having planned the same overt ovine operation.

By taking the path over Castle Hill and beneath Hartley it is possible to drop onto the river and head upstream into Stenkrith Park. Stuck between Kirkby and Nateby, Stenkrith is a natural wonderland. The vegetation grows only in competition with itself as the hustling Eden water rushes through. Channels of brockram rock rise and fall in ravines crashed and eroded by time to produce one of the most stunning local living

scenes. Proud of their Millennium and not satisfied with their woodland avenue downstream, the locals commissioned a new footbridge over the Eden, beneath the current road bridge. With the remains of the oldest bridge, believed to date from 1649, still visible by the edge of the gushing water, the Millennium construction re-visits man's passion to build bridges and the criss-cross of metal, stone and water engages.

Some books refer to it as Coup Keinan Hole and no doubt others modify the spelling still more. Dialect or slang terms, Cowcarn or Cow Canny bear their origins from the tale of a cow slipping and perishing unable to get out and are also easier to say. The warning to mind your step and retain a balance as the hurrying horizontal confuses the vertical stance is clear from a fifth name, the Devil's Mustard Mill.

In recent years the whole area above Stenkrith along the route of the old railway, has been renovated and made into an outstanding short walk over to Podgill Viaduct. If ghosts of dying animals on Bloody Bones Lane are all in the head,

The area is host to an interesting entry in the Eden Benchmark series of sculptures. Sequenced strategically down the length of the River Eden, "Passage" by Laura White is one of ten carved stone sculptures that also serve as seats. Like the bridge, the sculptures are a Millennium initiative. Like the bridge, they stimulate conversation and controversy in equal measure.

Brockram is also a complex structure being a concrete-like rock loaded with red sandstone, limestone and mud. Its cracks and crevices reveal tight chasms inviting you in, yet offering no immediate escape unless flat-bellied blind-eyed yoga navigation is a skill. The deeper of the holes rolling with splashing young Eden water, goes by the complex of Coopkarnel Hole, from the Danish equivalent for a 'cup shaped chasm'.

the sound of steel and the smell of steam are very real. It is nearly half a century since the line disappeared and yet the green flag waves and the whistle still blows for railway enthusiasts to gorge themselves on Kirkby Stephen's ubiquitous supply of transcendent transport. With railways in all directions the Kirkby visionaries even find space to add the Classic Commercial Vehicle Rally, which kicks off the calendar of the same name with a massive show at Easter.

The first sod of the Barnard Castle to Tebay line was cut at Kirkby Stephen on 25 August 1857. The line opened on 4 July 1861 and took vital traffic from Darlington to North Lancashire. From the paths and lanes above Kirkby Stephen a steady eye can still follow the contour of the railway as it loops through cuttings towards the junction at Tebay. We will continue our journey along these lines as I wave goodbye to my new friend Kirkby Stephen.

WAITBY SCHOOL

Scholarly life features through this book as I attempt to combine entertainment with education and vice versa. Attending Appleby County School from aged five to eleven I considered myself lucky to be amongst the same classmates for the duration, even though I knew no different - same age, same minds, same interests - comfort, to a degree. Indeed, to a large extent that same crowd then kept me company at Appleby Grammar School until I was eighteen. My Mam, rather unkindly I thought, was wont to tell me as a thirtysomething that this close-knit unit was thus responsible for my poor social skills. I dare not contest my mother's theory on social growth with my case in mind, yet with imagination I would suggest that many advanced life skills are learned in the closer school unit of a small class where the ages ranged in one room from five to eleven. This was the class at Waitby School. Debate no longer dictates the merits of such effective schooling as high finance and low government hold the chalk today.

At the junction for Waitby and Smardale sits Waitby School, which closed its doors to excitable, and one presumes well-behaved, children of these two hamlets in 1930. It clearly belongs to a different era and its walls must tell many a tale. Originally built in 1680 and restored 'by subscription' in 1867, it will no doubt go the way of many old buildings and fall into ruin. Unless of course, someone with the right capital and ambition can turn it into, what would be lovely, living quarters. The iconography of Waitby School mirrors the small-roomed derelict school at Raisbeck. Whilst their state of disrepair has remained relatively unchanged over the years, they cannot remain half-derelict forever and will sadly be too far from recovery soon. That invisible chorus of playground noise that echoes only at playtime will not even be a memory.

Waitby is a surprisingly interesting place. At the coupling of main street and back lane are typical layouts seen in Kirkby Stephen and Sedbergh on either side of the Howgill Fells. This does not mean that they are unique in this characteristic. Waitby shows evidence of 'town planning' and according to Roberts (*Five Westmorland Settlements*, CWAAS, 1993) it illustrates a twin back-lane system. Having had the luxury of two wells Waitby's two-toft compartments are suggested to be medieval in origin. Roberts even debates an arable green belt along the southern back lane.

The still-standing school offers a direct visual

aid to imagining the past, I struggle to find Waitby High Street and adjoining allotments possible even in my most vivid dreams and need a more distant gaze of imagination. Historians tell us that Waitby was once a market town with chapel, cemetery and castle. Its fame continues as the Waitby Dykes are well known across the country as one of the clearest dyke systems to illustrate settlements and ploughing remains. The chronologists have found the Waitby Dykes particularly useful in dating other settlements using knowledge of climatic trends and even details of ploughing standards married against the evidence 'on the ground' at Waitby.

SMARDALE VIADUCT

Smardale may be an odd place to extend a tour around the Howgills, as many may consider it to be outwith the Howgill umbrella - that controversy will run throughout the book - yet to me, it is a significant starting block for my countryside connections. Smardale has two viaducts and both have stories to tell. Call it anthropological; perhaps archaeological, sometime antiquarian, even artistically biased, this is where I first put pen to paper to describe my appreciation of our beautiful homeland. In 1975 I was "in print" having a letter in the oracular *Cumberland & Westmorland Herald*. This stimulated a short reciprocal public dialogue with a Mr Allonby who was able to add weight to my original missive. The correspondence went as follows:

"Sir, I would like to point out to your readers that 1975 is the centenary year of Smardale Viaduct, erected in 1875. If anyone should wish to see this brilliant masterpiece which, incidentally was built without the aid of machinery, they should be careful for the surrounding area contains

no signposts or directions of any kind. The best way is to go to Crosby Garrett, near Kirkby Stephen and turn left just past the schoolhouse; follow the road and it will lead you to the monument, which carries the London Midland railway. Yours, etc. Gareth Hayes, Appleby, March 15, 1975."

"Sir, May I add a little to Gareth Hayes' letter of last week and mention something of the history of Smardale Viaduct. Smardale, which has a dozen spans, is about 130 feet from stream to rails and has a length of 710 feet. It crosses over Scandal Beck and the old branch line from Kirkby Stephen to Tebay, the track of which has been removed. In sinking the foundations an unexpected difficulty arose. 'The river seemed to be running clear over solid rock, which at first sight seemed the ideal foundation' said the engineer 'We began to sink, but not a bit of rock was to be found. We had to go down 45 feet through clay till we came to red shale, and upon it we built'.

"The viaduct itself is erected of grey limestone

quarried locally about a mile up the valley. More than 60,000 tons of stone was used in the construction. The parapets and arch quoins are of millstone grit. The work of construction began in 1870 and occupied four and a half years. The last stone was secured into place in June of 1875, by Agnes Crossley (wife of the chief engineer, John S Crossley). As Gareth Hayes said last week, it is well worth a visit: standing majestic, dominating the surrounding picturesque countryside. It truly stands today as an everlasting monument to those who laboured on it and built it Yours, etc. J I Allonby, Crosby Garrett, 22 March 1975."

Smardale Viaduct continues to attract attention from railway lovers all over the world who come to visit the marvellous and spectacular Settle to Carlisle railway line. In October 2003 the viaduct was closed to rail traffic to allow important waterproofing exercises to be completed. Passengers had to take a coach service from Appleby to Garsdale while the work was undertaken. It is to the great credit of all concerned that the work was scheduled at all, as some years ago it was the disrepair of the line and the presumptive danger of the viaducts, particularly Batty Moss Viaduct at Ribblehead, that nearly closed the line altogether.

The other railway line from Kirkby Stephen to Tebay out of Kirkby Stephen East did not survive. Closed in 1960, one hundred years after it first opened, the line does however now offer a form of rebirth for the enthusiast and nature lover. This time it is not as a railway, your imagination will have to suffice for that thrill, but as a superb walk. Smardale Gill takes advantage of a three and a half mile stretch of the old railway, passing under Smardale Viaduct on the active Settle to Carlisle line. Designated a Site of Special Scientific Interest, Cumbria Wildlife Trust has maintained parts of the area since 1978 and now through realised growth opportunities looks after around one hundred acres of one of the loveliest and best kept secrets of Cumbria. The site was declared a National Nature Reserve in 1997 so word must be getting around. The name Smardale is derived from the dell of the smere, the clover.

The disused Smardale viaduct of the South Durham and Lancashire Union Railway was opened in 1860 after a design by Thomas Bouch, who went on to receive fame, but perhaps not with popularity, as the designer behind the Tay Bridge. Bouch made two significant mistakes with the

Tay Bridge. He omitted to make an error calculation to account for estuary winds and, through lack of supervision, allowed the builders to use sub-standard material. The collapse of the main section on a stormy night in December 1879 was the end of Bouch but not, thankfully, the end of the stone-built Smardale viaduct. In 1990 some 30 years after the line had closed the bridge was repaired thanks to the efforts of the Northern Viaduct Trust, which had been formed in 1986. The Trust continues to do good work on the line having recently repaired and re-decked Podgill Viaduct on the other side of Kirkby Stephen thus creating the splendid pathway from Stenkrith Park.

It is easy to confuse the two neighbourly viaducts when entering conversation although this, according to my walking companion Bob Parmley, is a simple distinction made by gender. He says 'Smardale viaduct has a king pier which makes it masculine whereas Smardale Gill viaduct does not, making it feminine'. Clearly.

To the west of the viaduct are the remnants of two large commercial lime kilns. Repaired to respectable condition they stand proud as statues to an age never to return. The lime kilns were responsible for producing the lime to make mortar for the construction of the viaduct and it is great testimony to the engineers of both constructions that they still stand proud today. Just beyond the lime kilns is a path down to Scandal Beck and another, the original, Smardale Bridge. In the warm summer months this is an ideal setting for reflection and if the mood demands the waters of the Scandal can be refreshing too.

The continuing trackbed from Smardale runs through a fine cutting, hidden completely from view from all roads and most walks. Dry stonewalls support Sandybank Cutting as they did a century ago. Self-draining they curve out of sight and conjure up incredible memories of a railway age. Rumbling train moving slowly because of the corner, cut and clearing ahead pours smoke and steam down and beneath steel wheels and heavy load. Abandoned in time, a gentle stroll down this cutting is really now no different to rambling around stone circles, over earth barrows and other such ancient sites. At Sandybank Signal Box, where some remains cling to a grassy knoll, double track took over for the downhill run to Tebay and the path clearly doubles in width. The route heads down to Newbiggin-on-Lune and the railway trackbed disappears as it serves to give the main trunk road its home from here to Tebay.

The natural route from Smardale to the next port of call is not obvious, as it does not appear to lie on any obvious path. North, south, with river,

is the narrow twist required to turn through it. Portly people should take heed likewise. The challenge will hopefully lead to laughter rather than hopeless frustration. The route heads up and over Crosby Garrett Scar, Orton Scar and the open moor. It's the route that has been taken by many of our ancestors whose footsteps have long since been lost since the turnpike road linked Orton to Appleby via Hoff Lunn. The drove roads from Scotland are at cross-purposes to today's diagonals. Hidden valleys with relics of homesteads devoid of maintenance and yet with occasional good company as the fells do see like-minded walkers and outdoor types keen to seek fresh air. Nettle Hill, Beacon Hill and Greystones are a short rise from Severals and, if the weather's good, give some of the best views from the lowland scars. The Pennine range to the east is complimented by Green Bell and Randygill of the Howgills in the south and when bathed in sun, they give tremendous comfort like protecting

with road, with rail, it depends on needs. Kirkby Stephen or Appleby or Tebay may be options highlighted because of the presence of the railway, and indicative of the last century's priorities. Walking along the trackbed it is tempting and no less desirable to play trains and carry straight on towards Newbiggin-on-Lune. If opportunity allows, derail yourself onto Begin Hill and the Severals. Be warned! The kissing gate is not rucksack friendly such

arms around a newborn baby. The foreground view is equally enticing showing the criss-crossing railway lines, old and new, and the rolling hidden valleys glorious whatever the season. From either Newbiggin-on-Lune or the car park at Smardale, this is an easy walk and suits anyone whose limit is a couple of miles.

The route is popular but never busy. You may meet a handful of hearty souls and acknowledge honest greetings; you will certainly see a distant farmer, dog and quad-bike out working; you may even engage in whistling reflections with high skylarks. It may be contradictory to call it friend-ly solitude, yet that is exactly what it is and it sits very nicely on my shoulders, thank you. If a hundred miles and more is a distance more your style then the same route offers an opportunity to join Wainwright's Coast-to-Coast walk. Well-sign-posted, well-worn, and well-worth joining.

Men lived here as a community where no men now live and few men ever come. A gap in our knowledge of the early settlers in the district might well be bridged by expert excavation of the site. The principal site, Severals, covers three acres; there are two others immediately to the north, the whole area of occupation extending

over an area of 100 acres. A modern wall divides the settlements and a stile in it is used to pass through the main site on a descending slope to a disused railway track, which is crossed to reach Smardale Bridge in a lovely unfrequented valley containing other prehistoric remains, these of a different type, but probably once associated with life at Severals.

A Wainwright, *Wainwright's Coast to Coast*, 1987

POTTS VALLEY AND SUNBIGGIN TARN

The valley that runs alongside Smardale on one side and before the expanse of Orton Scar is Potts Valley, home to secret and stunning scenery. Potts Valley is considered so special that the Friends of the Lake District have now acquired it as an area of outstanding beauty and one to be preserved. It will be protected as a haven of wildlife whether animal or beast, plant or stony outcrop. The 1,500 acres of Little Asby Common, which includes Potts Valley was purchased by the Friends in late 2002 and may be one of their most important acquisitions.

Founded in 1934 the Friends is a charitable body that exists with high values aimed at promoting the natural elements of the Lake District and Cumbria, and in doing so takes appropriate action to protect the landscape. The geological

importance of this area cannot be underestimated and it is world renowned because of its limestone pavements. Accepted global nomenclature for the timing of geological formations is usually taken from where the first estimations were taken. The term Asbian, from Asby, reflects any geological feature that came about some 340 million years ago. Thus any dated rocks of this era found anywhere in the world will be known as from the Asbian Period.

These low bleak fells would have been trapped between the ice sheets of the larger Pennine and Lake District ranges during the ice age. The glaciers moved picking up huge pieces of pink Shap granite and depositing them, like pebbles falling out of a rolling snowball, across the scar and down the Eden Valley. These granite erratics are as unique as the limestone pavements and often confuse unknowing visitors in believing they were placed by stone-aged man. According to the Friends' quarterly journal, current geological thinking is that Potts Valley had its own special origin. It is thought that it was formed when the Howgill Fells drained into the Eden rather than the Lune. When the Lune later took the waters from the Howgills a large deep valley was left with just the tiny Potts Beck to run through it.

My first visit to Potts Valley was with a rowdy, yet enthusiastic, mini-bus load of teenagers on an 'O' level biology field trip. Our teacher was keen himself and I think, I hope, we gave him more pleasant memories than troubled ones. 'Turry from Furryhill' was one of the kinder nicknames that I expect have now gone downstream as he now goes by the title of Mr. Hobson, headteacher, Appleby Grammar School. We threw our quadrants across wild grass and knelt to count and record our findings. We also threw them high to see them bounce over limestone hollows. Potts Beck was so still and beautiful that spring day that the fresh air raised the spirits and the silly season was upon us. We laughed at the names for the outcrops high above us and even now in my advancing years I can still find amusement in the innuendo titled Windy Banks and Willycock Stones.

The fields, walls and waterways challenged us to Olympian feats of dare. My biggest leap across the meandering Potts Beck may have been long but it was not long enough as I hit the bank so squarely I had no option but to sit straight back

down like a triple-jumper falling back into the sand-pit. The chill water immediately cooled any embarrassment. Luckily it was nearly time for home and the light blue Ford Transit minibus that lived its life in such devotion did not complain about my damp behind. I do know that one of the reasons we visited Potts Beck was because of its thriving native crayfish population which thrived in the unpolluted limey beck. Worryingly, the Friends report that this species is now under threat from crayfish plague carried by the non-native Signal crayfish. Alarmingly they also report that the plague can wipe out entire populations. If validity was required for their purchase of the land, this alone should be it.

On a recent walk across this fell I came across a three-foot high electric fence splitting the fell in two as a stock-line for the grazing sheep. The walker may have cause to grimace as he arrives where there is no gate; this is sure indication that he has followed a sheep-track and not the permissive path as outlined on the Ordnance Survey map. How permanent these fences will be is unclear. The yellow warning signs are usually only temporary and can often be found lying upside in mud or dust. That may be my unsubtle warning against an impatient attempt to straddle the fence. It was a dare of youthful days to reach out and, with one finger, touch the fence. The recoiling spring from the ground tended to be a premeditated vaulted precaution rather than a pulsating volted performance.

Sunbiggin Tarn is known to locals as a little oasis to sit near and catch up with private thoughts. To field observers and naturalists it is well known as a site to observe rare species of bird and fowl, and take delight in identifying favourite flowers and plant life. The tarn is a mixture of 'reed bed, sedge swamp and mossy lawns of lime flushes'. Unless you are an enthusiast you may be better off not straying too close to the

boggy edge, for flies and midges take no prisoners, but rather to sit peacefully just off the higher road. From this viewpoint, the panorama of Howgill Fells changes colour before your very eyes as shadows lengthen and the inevitability of the end of the day draws forth. The water drains out of the tarn at the southern end and gives us a lovely example of our flowing terminology, as Tarn Sike becomes Rais Beck, which in turn gives itself to the mother river the Lune.

The roads around Sunbiggin are narrow six-foot wide affairs and during the summer of 2003 they were closed preventing passers-by from sampling Sunbiggin or stretching weary souls in the soft summer sunshine. Our administrative boffins in their European offices had decreed that the shallow bridges, no more than weighty hardcore concrete and tight tarmac over narrow pipes, had to be reinforced to enable them to withstand 40 tonne trucks. Apart from the unlikelihood of such vehicles reaching these roads, the cattle grids standing guard to Little Asby Fell were not on the Eurolists and consequently were not reinforced; they may just struggle with a juggernaut, should one come along.

The tarn itself contains several different species of trout, some of which grow to a considerable size. For those who enjoy open spaces, fine scenery, and the sight and sounds of birds, this is one of the most attractive spots in North Westmorland. It is here, according to the Rev. Hodgson ('History of Westmorland', 1820), that while digging peats, about 1730, 'two pairs of bull's horns, joined together in the posture of fighting', were found.

F B Chancellor, *Around Eden*, 1954

NEWBIGGIN-ON-LUNE

Traffic speeds by ignoring a lovely little hamlet and amputating a limb of houses as it cuts a path on the pacey road pretending to be a railway for the next few short miles to Tebay. The old railway station is among this broken limb of stones now restored to a very fine residential array. In active life this was known as Ravenstonedale Station to avoid confusion with all the other Newbiggins in the country. My United Kingdom atlas gives me more than 20 Newbiggins (and no Oldbiggins!). However, confusion may not have been avoided as Kirkby Stephen Station was once called Kirkby Stephen and Ravenstonedale Station (over a mile from Kirkby Stephen and three miles from Ravenstonedale). In the days of the railway when communication was perhaps slower (but more efficient) I doubt if many people alighted at

Ravenstonedale Station expecting to get off in the centre of Ravenstonedale. Fellow passengers would have used that old fashioned tool of conversation to give ample warning of the station's location.

Incidentally, the name Newbiggin has its own varieties of origin. One of the simplest being that the word Biggin is short for 'beginning' and refers to the start of the new settlement or village. Another explanation involves the French word *beguine* or a praying woman (the term *béguinage* or *begijnhof* is used in the low countries for religious almshouses for women). However, the most likely origin is that it simply means a building, and we are left with many 'new biggins' (i.e. new buildings) up and down the country.

Further back from the road is Tower House (by Brownber Hall, the stately care home for the elderly in the manner of Stobars). Tower House was former home to Elizabeth Gaunt the last woman to be burnt at the stake for a political crime and the last woman to be burnt at the famous Tyburn site in London in 1685. Her story is worth telling.

Elizabeth Gaunt was the Anabaptist daughter of wealthy and prominent figure, Anthony Fothergill. It is only in the last decade that the Fothergills have left their home of so many uninterrupted years. Perhaps because of her upbringing Elizabeth tended to have a 'charitable' nature and, linked to her beliefs, was known to help the needy. The Anabaptists were a group of English Dissenters originally founded in Europe who attributed little importance to theological consideration but placed high value on the Word of God and love for their fellow man. The word Anabaptist derives from the Greek meaning re-baptism and was illustrated by the patterns of adult baptisms.

Based on their radical social beliefs Anabaptists joined many non-conformist sects by being persecuted by the civil authorities, their dissenting cause being denounced by Luther, Calvin, Zwingli, the Protestant and Catholic Church. However charitable, Elizabeth Gaunt was going to be paddling against a political tide particularly as this was the punishing period of Judge Jeffreys. Born in Wales, Judge George Jeffreys is famously known as Hanging Judge Jeffreys, yet his penal sentences were not limited to the noose.

Burning at the stake in public was the penalty for heresy and witchcraft, but also in the case of women alone, it was used for those convicted of high treason or petty treason. Men who were convicted of high treason were hanged, drawn and quartered but this was not appropriate for women, as it would have involved nudity! A fascinating moral conflict. High treason offences included counterfeiting and the clipping of coins for pieces of silver and gold known as 'coining'. An example of a petty treason crime was the murder by a woman of her husband.

Elizabeth Gaunt harboured and cared for the political activist James Burton, when he was wanted for his part in the Rye House assassination plot. She later helped him escape the country to Amsterdam. On his return, to save his own 'neck' he gave her to the authorities and she was denied strangulation and ordered by Jeffreys to be burned at the stake for high treason. According to the records, Elizabeth Gaunt displayed 'peculiar manners and phraseology' and this was put down to the fashions of her sect. I rather think it may have been partly due to her soft Westmorland dialect.

She had also written a 'graceful paper' at the time of her execution, which was received with compassion and horror by the thousands who read it. She forgave her captors and left them to the judgement of the King of Kings. Quaker William Penn, campaigner for peace and truth, attended the public execution, having rushed from a hanging at Cheapside, and wrote 'when she calmly disposed the straw about her in such a manner as to shorten her sufferings, all the bystanders burst into tears'. Since that day, no woman has been executed for a political offence.

The Anabaptists grew from other dissenters of the time such as the Brownists, Barrowists, Waldenses, Wycliffites and Lollards; the family tree of non-conformity is as intriguing as it can be complex. The Anabaptists are often more commonly known now as Baptists or Brethren or variations upon words that are more clearly understood today. Somehow the casual term 'simple chapel folk' implied by 'Brethren' betrays their roots of persecution and their long struggle to be allowed to follow a simple doctrine within the authoritarian higher church. Yet, their strength, faith and hope is worthy of admiration.

Non-conformity itself is an intriguing description and can make pre-judgements on personality and goal. Essentially deriving from the 17th century it was first used during the Penal Acts after the Restoration of 1660 and the Act of Uniformity of 1662 where descriptions were made of the places of worship (the Conventicles) of the Separatist congregations. The term Dissenters used in parallel was first used to name the 'Five Dissenting Brethren' at the Westminster Assembly of Divines in 1644-47.

Applying the word non-conformist today can bring miscomprehension. Whether rebellious revolutionaries or hippy headcases there may be a value. The most obvious dissenter of today is the ecofriend who fears for the survival of the planet. Of course, one can work hard at preserving our earth without looking like we have been just dragged out of it. Even the non-conformists of the 17th century would have an outlook on appearance in their marketing plan.

On the southern side of the road lies the heart of

the village. Newbiggin Lune Spring Garden Centre has an excellent garden centre, antique shop, furniture makers and cafe - a strange 'nonconformist' turn on the multifunctional retail mall. The antique shop is even unmanned and kindly requests that departing customers switch off the light. I am not so sure about the garden ornaments of hedgehog, rabbit, gnomes with wheelbarrows, that guard the door to the antique and furniture making rooms. Moving away from the building to the grounds, I cannot dispute owner and nurseryman Norman Ousby's fair claim of, 'If it'll grow here it'll grow anywhere'.

The village centre is a collection of lovely picturesque properties and even the old chapel of St. Aidan's has been converted into a charming cottage. The one remaining place of worship is the Methodist Church, which rather uncomfortably sits right by the by-pass and architecturally does not help signpost a pretty village. Built in 1939, its manner depicts that era, yet somehow it now provides a suitable architectural stepping-stone as we move from the busy new road into the ancient village centre. There is fun to be had here by trying to identify buildings that have changed their use from the original purpose. Try and spot the old Primitive Methodist Chapel or St. Aidan's.

Curiosities continue as you peel your eyes around the buildings of Low House and the mill next door, and see faces carved into the side of one house. Sculptured by a visiting Italian they were presumably commissioned and give an indication of the wealth in this region. They are not, as you may expect, carvings of local landlords but the faces of the pop stars of the day: politicians Gladstone and Disraeli, and female icons Queen Victoria and Florence Nightingale. As old buildings are seconded into secular use (others are school, cobblers, bakery and candle factory, and of course the railway station on the other side of the main road) the wealth still remains yet the nature of the market has changed.

Pass by too quickly and a double take may be necessary as you think you imagine a boat in a field. It is in a field but it's also in a small lake; one of three belonging to the Bessy Beck Trout Farm. Opened nearly 20 years ago by Vera Balantyne who at the time of writing is on her way to the Shetland Isles (and more water) and passing the business over to the good hands of

Shelley Riddell. Bessy Beck is thought by some to be named after Elizabeth 'Bessy' Gaunt and there is a fair supposition that she must have used the waters of the beck prior to her travels. There are tales of a 'presence' in the air by the water's edge as if Bessy has returned home to drink from her stream. The mood cannot be too scary as people return from all over the world to attempt to lure Bessy's trout.

RAISBECK AND KELLETH

Avoiding the old railway new road, the more pleasant route west out of Newbiggin is back on the higher lane towards Kelleth. The route follows the contour line parallel to the faster valley road and is all the more peaceful for it. Offering a bird's eye view of the immediate valley, it allows the whole of the northern range of Howgill Fells to come into view. And what a vista. Seemingly stretching for miles it goes up and up and up, to a broad horizon of peaks at last resembling Wainwright's elephants in herd.

If the elephants turn mermaids and entice, there are a number of ways across and up to satisfy the temptation. Wath, by definition, is a hamlet around a water crossing yet the modern age has somewhat diminished the original usage. The water crossing is practically drowned in scale now by the large flat bridge of the impatient A685. The underpass bridge is a lowly eight feet high and must be a challenge for many agricultural vehicles, which seem to get larger themselves as years advance. Bowderdale, Weasdale and Cotegill combine both cul-de-sac and gateway to those with boots and lofty ambition.

Back on the terrace towards Kelleth and at the roadside are a number of large lime kilns. These icons of the period were built during the agricultural revolution of the 18th century. However, lime kilns were first seen in Britain in Roman times when limestone was burnt to produce a mortar for building. When it was discovered that lime reduced the acidity of the soil by raising the pH vast numbers of kilns were erected and many can still be seen today by roadsides on the edge of ridges throughout Cumbria. Farmers would build their own for seasonal use and although this may seem extravagant it is no different to building a field house or sheepfold.

Limestone when burnt turns from calcium carbonate into calcium oxide, commonly known as quick lime. The addition of water produces calcium hydroxide or slaked lime, which is then spread on the land. The lime kilns along the Kelleth road are the simple forms where limestone and fuel were placed in alternate layers; as the burning combination was drawn up the chimney of the kiln the burnt lime could be taken out at the bottom. Simple and very effective. These architectural oddities are both photogenic and a vital and visible memory of farm life not too long ago. Many are intact only losing a few stones to supplement dry stonewall repair. The commercial kilns were much larger, like the ones at Smardale and tended to be run continuously. New fans of lime kilns may want to retrace their steps to Newbiggin where there is a huge double-sided kiln.

Access to these lime kilns is limited by farmland and this is probably wise as they are clearly structures in crumbling decay. It may not be long

Honeyed Seal of soft affections,
Tenderest pledge of future bliss,
Dearest tie of young connections,
Love's first snowdrop, virgin kiss.

One of the best features of the Cumbrian landscape is not to have to comply with the fee required at National Trust properties, or indeed English Heritage, as we have plenty of hidden gems of floral displays. If we know where they are. We do. Bluebell woods litter woodland in the region and snowdrops too. In particular, the snowdrops at Raisbeck are outstanding and with a roadside location in full sun backdropped by aged trees and dry stonewall they truly capture the spirit and intent of Burns' romantic vision. Bearing the family name Galanthus - from the Greek *gala* meaning milk, and *anthos* for flower - the snowdrop was brought

before they are all acquired by national bodies of natural intent and fenced in with a pay box and assistant to take your money to view.

Many National Trust properties contain grounds and gardens, which have superb spreading displays of snowdrops from mid or late January (depending on the local climate). These displays are a welcome sign that spring is finally on its way and perhaps that is why snowdrops are generally viewed with a special fondness. The same appreciation of nature is seen with bluebells in May as summer takes its hold. Both give us blankets of colour and a canvas for joy. Robert Burns used our mental image of new life and perception of snowdrop beginning to great effect:

to Britain in Roman times and we will see later in the book that a significant Roman presence was only five miles away.

The snowdrops provide a perfect compliment of new life and innocence to the small school building on the other side of the road. Whilst it is practically derelict, the old Whitehead school is still a very beautiful building. I have called it the Whitehead School, as that is a passing term I have heard used, and records show a Mrs Alice Whitehead as one of the teachers during the mid-19th century and, of course, the Whitehead's are a Raisbeck family. The age of the building should not be allowed to go unnoticed for it was built in 1780. Sources tell us that the 'Yeoman farmers' and 'Freeholders' of Raisbeck and the hamlet of Sunbiggin erected the school for the purposes of educating the farm children in the ways of the Bible.

Almost perfectly square, the tiny building was used for its original purpose until the late 1890s when presumably the turnpike roads offered a fast route to larger schools at Orton, Tebay and beyond. Significantly, the most relevant history of the schoolhouse is more recent. Barely two decades ago, in the spring of 1982 the building had fallen into a dangerous state and demolition was planned with immediate effect. In stepped local character and author of some note, Michael Ffinch who was able to bend over backwards and twist the right number of arms to save the building.

Ffinch was a man of some stature and the building was not only saved but also fully restored with the help of the Historic Buildings Commission. Whether this was done by high or low politics is irrelevant now as the small schoolhouse is still with us.

Warning words must beckon however as the building will not take care of itself. Michael Ffinch had illustrated his passion for the school by dedicating a poem, 'The Dame School at Raisbeck', in his *Westmorland Poems* (Titus Wilson 1983) and then in a special edition limited run of only fifty copies called simply *The Dame School of Raisbeck* (Titus Wilson 1984). In the latter work he briefly described the above tale and dates his poem as being written in 1980. Had the powers that be decided to demolish it a decade earlier or a decade later then I think we can be sure that the building would no longer be with us. Certainly it was a quirk of fate that prompted a

Just below the brow to the steadings of Raisbeck, over Slapestone Bridge, is the Raisbeck Pinfold Cone, part of Cumbria's rural sculptural art project 'Sheepfolds'. International sculptor Andy Goldsworthy is the visionary behind the project taking desolated sheepfolds and rebuilding or repairing them for the public's enjoyment and as a natural memorial to rural times. Hailing from Brough, Andy Goldsworthy has achieved worldwide acclaim and, while the planned construction of a hundred sheepfolds stuttered because of foot and mouth in 2001, there is no doubting the tourist value of his agricultural monuments.

work of faith. The poem, like many of its ilk, is a long one yet I cannot resist giving you a taster from the first few lines to whet your appetite for more of Ffinch's work.

Out in the wide open, these performances of Public Art are clearly sighted and cited as regeneration of a derelict landscape. I don't know if Andy Goldsworthy will look at other field corners to visit the wrecked barns for more artistic creativity.

> *By drystone walls on Raisbeck Green*
> *A square stone cottage can be seen*
> *Whose gaping front and slate-torn roof*
> *Have long since ceased to weatherproof*
> *And yet its upright chimney might*
> *Still draw a flame towards the light*
> *But for the stunted sapling rowan*
> *The cottage guards the Green alone*
> *Thoughtfully placed where five ways meet*
> *A butt against the hail and sleet*
> *Shelter for hikers, lovers' scrawls*
> *Are pencilled on its peeling walls*
> *Yet few who note the rafters' groans*
> *Will know what children stirred these stones*
> *Along the lanes of Raisbeck once*
> *Came scholar, dreamer, idler, dunce*
> *From Sunbiggin and Stony Head*
> *Small boys, and girls, big sister-led*

farmers. Sadly, a minority of farmers let their colleagues down by turning that corner into a rubbish pit which is not only ugly but serves as a danger to the public and the wildlife around. This is a slight digression on Goldsworthy yet adds to the debate of what is natural and what is manmade and what, therefore, is true countryside?

I do know that as an artform it brings revenue into the region and this must be good.

In a similar fashion to trying to see all the Eden Benchmark series, many people like to go sheepfold spotting treating them as a collectable. It suits the people who do not take to the hobbiest extremes of climbing every Munro or spending their days sitting on Platform 4 of Carlisle Station. The sheepfolds are very photogenic yet incredibly difficult to photograph well. We should not forget that the remaining derelict sheepfolds are also extremely photogenic and their slow dissolution into the landscape is as much a memorial to the shepherding of days gone by, as is the regeneration by Goldsworthy. He may move onto barn roofs and field houses and especially, he may move onto lime kilns and I hope he does. I also hope he does it in moderation.

Regular walkers will notice the discarded farm machinery left to ruin and rust in the corner of fields by the custodians of the countryside, the

ORTON

The name Orton derives from Overton, and sometimes Over-Rigg. Some ancient records give it distinction by calling it Sker Overton to reflect it as belonging to the rocky open land, the 'scar', under which it sits. Orton is a village made of corners. Viewing it from the scar, on a clear day, it resembles a tight street map laid out on a rug or large board for kids and their Matchbox toys. There appears to be three routes to get to anywhere in the triangular harmony of ins, outs, and sharp turns. Modern icons dominate today's village, as motorway users take a pit stop to satisfy their thirsts. The necessity for bright colours does not go unnoticed by Mad Monks Music Shop. Their name hardly needs a luminous purple sign. The Chocolate Factory has been in Orton longer and makes a very fine attempt at increasing the waistline of visitors who prefer to exercise their wallets to their limbs. In many years to come, anthropological authors will ponder the social-economics of a small village and its shops of chocolate and guitars

Close to the motorway and a mere 20 minutes from Kendal or Penrith, Orton has plenty of choice in nearby supermarkets should the shopper have the need and means of transport. Yet, there is a bland duplicity about supermarkets today. They no longer deserve the pretext 'super' and some would say the free choice offered by the word 'market' is loosely applied as the chain of super and now, hypermarkets monopolise and brainwash the customer through aggressive and subliminal advertising.

It seems contradictory to say that we have lost a great deal in having everything available when we want it, yet I sometimes feel this is true. Global seasonality has taken away the magical anticipation of our delightful harvest. Sadly, I fear the taste has gone too. Who really wants a cucumber that doesn't make you burp or an onion that doesn't make you cry? Throughout the country the Farmer's Market is attempting to cut out the fat-cat middlemen supplying the supermarkets. Devoted to fresh, local produce, there is no doubting the return of the taste too. It has often rained when I have been to Orton's Farmer Market. It says something about the spirit of the traders and their customers that weather does not hold them back.

Orton was granted a market charter by Edward I in 1271 and continues the market tradition with a well-advertised, well-attended and well-admired Farmers Market. Conceived and run by Jane Brook and Greg Wilson the Orton Farmer's Market is truly the pioneer of Farmer's Markets. The first market was held in the Market Hall (built by public subscription around 1865) in May 2000 when twelve stallholders offered their wares to around 200 customers. By late 2003 the market had spread outside to cope with the 38 stalls and 1500 visitors.

Orton Farmers' Market was announced overall winner of the farmers' markets awards for 2003 at the National Conference in Edinburgh on 19 November. It was presented with the award by Clarissa Dickson-Wright who has promised to come and visit the market in person soon.

Its success is down to the determination of Jane and Greg to make sure that it retains its core values in local produce. As such they run strict controls on quality and sourcing for the enthusiastic stallholders. In their words, 'All produce must be grown, reared, caught, brewed, pickled, baked, smoked or processed by the stall holder' and in the case of crafts, all 'goods must be made by the stallholder and use materials sourced locally wherever possible'. At the very least, ten per cent of the produce on offer must be sourced locally and all sellers must be from within a 50 miles radius of Orton.

This apparent broad brush is actually quite tight and is strictly observed. In the event over 60 per cent of the stalls come from a 20 mile radius of Orton and Jane and Greg regularly visit stallholders on site to check their advertising claims. For example they like to be assured that claims under the sign 'organic' are supported by certification from the Soil Association. The market organisation leads with its own high values and is registered as a 'not for profit community business'.

In June 2002, Orton Farmers' Market celebrated by becoming the first certified member of the National Association of Farmers' Markets (NAFM). It has already secured a turbulent history of highlights having enjoyed a visit by Prince Charles in January 2001 and then survived the temporary closure caused by foot and mouth during the rest of that year. During 2003 the atmosphere bubbled with global surrealism as live music from around the world performed at the market with welcome affection. Unlikely combos such as the Segretta Stompers (albeit based in Carlisle), the Black Sheep Morris Dancers and the Kirkby Stephen Silver Band (er, based in Kirkby Stephen), Kausary (Andes music from London), the Hi-Tech Steel Band (from Manchester of course), and the Rhythm Kings New Orleans Jazz Band (based where else but Dumfries), the Cherrypickers Steel Band (Manchester), and the Doghouse Skiffle Band (had to be from Hull) have all been listed as live events and prove without a shadow of a doubt that there can be

unity with diversity.

Curiously, and this is a damnation of the stereotypical salesman, by having a 'people-who-make-are-the-people-who-sell' outlook there is a friendly and trustworthy spirit to the market. And variety? Game, sausage, and traditionally reared lamb, beef and pork are to be expected. As too are fruit and vegetables, assorted plants, and poultry and preserves. There is also cheese and more cheese, butter, buttermilk and fish, and not all from Bessy Beck! Fruit cordials and microbrewery beverages, and tea or coffee in the back room of the Market Hall... and more, with equal imagination.

Jane Barker sells compost as a Fine Purveyor of Manure. Dianne Halliday comes from Mallerstang to sell cakes and traybakes and is a fine example of farmer diversification. She is even planning tourist paragliding as an additional income. The wood turner presents his goods with the unique warning sign saying 'Please Touch'. Kath Hoffman designs and produces her craft cards with a unique style. I have to add that it was my prompt that got her doing the superb character sheep. Flat Jacques entertains with speciality pancakes and a global appreciation of blini, crepe, pannekoeke, flaeskpannkaka and po-ping. Finally, although the list could go on, Broughton Bread offers the early customer (you have to be quick) a breathtaking bundle of bread including walnut, tomato and basil, mature cheddar, parmesan and herb, sunflower seed, sun-dried tomato and olive, cheese and chive, mixed seed, pumpkin seed, sage and onion, sweet potato and cheese, and wheat free, not to mention the sweet breads of cranberry and hazelnut, and apricot and almond.

Orton has a pride and rightly so. In May 2002 the Coronation Shelter (built to commemorate Queen Elizabeth's in 1953) was renovated and given a bright cheerful interior thanks to the efforts of the village's children. Twelve kids took proper plans and paint to decorate the bus shelter interior in vivid countryside greens, yellows and blues. The sunny local views depicted brighten any reason to use the shelter. The people of Orton have one of the finest, if not the finest, community spirits in the region.

Orton is full of old curiosities and not all are made of bricks and mortar. It has many weird and wonderful tales of mystery and intrigue. The Methodee Man (Methodist minister) was hired to rid the village of the Orton Boggle. The assumption being that the Methodee man would have powers of exorcism similar to those reserved for the Catholic priests. Methodee Man was no super-hero and when his hat blew off and hit him in his own face he departed without addressing the Boggle. Sawrey's *History of Orton* (1967) mentions a Cooper House Boggle known for making strange knocking sounds and flinging cutlery about. I am not sure if the Orton Boggle and the Cooper House Boggle are the same spirit. Another spirit went by the name of Marian yet having 'served her time' she is now at rest. There is another tale of a human skull, being used as a nail box, bringing a succession of bad luck until the local joiner sealed it into in a wooden box under the stairs. If you ever wondered what was

in that box under the stairs...

All Saints watches over its parishioners in a Dibley-like manner and I expect the people who sit in chamber to organise and care for this homely community also mirror the diverse characterisations of the popular BBC comedy series. The church tower bravely peaks over the whole of the village as a beacon to draw visitors for warm invitation and due protection. As well as the market hall in the main square (or triangle), All Saints acts as host to many events throughout the year and is a superb vessel for good village life.

George Whitehead, (1636-1723) one of the founder members of the Quakers, was from Orton and was instrumental in the radical changes that led to the Quaker rights expressed in the Magna Carta of 1696. George Whitehead is often confused with the Calvinistic co-founder of the Methodist Church, George Whitefield (1714-1770). It is easy to see why. With similar names and with few years separation Whitefield pioneered Field Preaching with John Wesley and many must have assumed parallels with George Fox and the Quaker Movement.

Whitehead's influence was to bring a dawn of Quietism to the Quaker Way. George Fox, Francis Howgill, James Nayler and others had battled with the turbulent times of the 17th century to raise the profile of the Quakers and profound Dissent, yet much of this dynamic was a challenge to their beliefs of humility and a gentle way. Whitehead was able to soften the cause. In other words he realised he could not change the world, but he and his church had won the right to exist. Quietism, and indeed, Pluralism, was born in this period and a son of Orton can take credit. They might not know it, they certainly do not need to know it, but the people of Orton still portray some of George Whitehead's spiritual gift.

Driving in and out of Orton is a thrill from any direction. From Tebay, kids whoop with delight as a big dipper ride past the road ends to Coatflatt sends the stomach high and the jaw low. Out of Orton towards the scar and the great climb past Bullflatt onto the scar is a challenge to the grip on the gear stick and a test of timing, especially if following slower traffic. Taking it the other way is even better. Starting from the scar, the views of Orton in the foreground and our Howgill tops in the distance surely compete with the best in the World. Yes, the World! Different every time, it still sends a shiver down my back. Oh, and don't expect to see Orton if you are travelling early in the morning. The Orton fog lies very low and with the tower of All Saints peeking through, the eye is more than satisfied. Coming out the other side the big dipper thrills once more. However, please treat this drive with extreme caution as people drive too quickly through Orton. With impatience and habit on the agenda the chicane past the bus shelter and George Hotel must be treated with care and respect. Slow down.

With the advent of motors and the improved forms of locomotion the places of beauty off the beaten track of the railways, are coming into something of the former glory of the coaching days. There are a vast number of people, and the number is ever increasing, who desire to see the nooks and corners of the country. The development in the last few years in this direction is very noticeable. Orton is situated on the main Appleby to Kendal road and each entry and exit gives a commanding view of great beauty. Those who travel along that road are amply repaid. The scenery is picturesque and the road over the fell country is good. Such panoramic views are rarely met or seldom equalled. The country is full of points of interest and absorbing scenes. When travelling along the road the feeling is borne in upon one, 'That it is good to be where God is great and man is small'

Harold Sawrey, *700+ Orton - History of a Country Parish*, 1967.

ORTON SCAR OVER TO ODDENDALE

At first glance Orton Scar is something to escape from. The wind blows and there is no shelter from the weather, whether it is heavy rain or beaming sun. The barren landscape gives sheep a home but not man, except for a cluster of cottages at Coalpit Hill and the wonderful Gaythorne Hall hidden below the narrow road to Great Asby. Gaythorne Hall is memorable in recent times for portraying the titular mansion to the successful BBC television production of Anne Bronte's *The Tenant of Wildfell Hall*. Wild fell is an appropriate name and the high red tipped tops on black and white posts that run by the roads give good measure to the potential of drifting snow. Contrary to my wild weather warning a trek across the scar is very much worth the effort. An abundance of wild life in their habitat, not ours, humbles as much as it extrapolates the knowledge and exercises the knees.

Each road across the scar seems to rise to the horizon and disappear over the top into the unknown and is reminiscent of road and horizon on the poster for the 1970s science fiction block-buster film *Close Encounters of the Third Kind* with the tag line 'We Are Not Alone'. Indeed alien landings on the open moor would lead them to perceive something radically different of Earth than if they landed in the monochrome city sprawls of nearby Carlisle or Lancaster.

Open roads with no walls or fences or hedges like this offer an odd freedom. It is not the open road of Route 66 in vast America, which I find much too big for satisfactory empathy. It is not the open road of one of our motorways at 4am on a summer's morning as their beauty is simply a surreal snapshot on a heavy rolled concrete strip of death. It is more intimate than that. It combines scales, large and small, and transcends time, past with present. Only the future is unclear. How ironic then that I compare its vision with that of a futuristic cinema experience. It gives me the freedom and space, escapism brimming with emptiness and untenanted saturation. Unquestionably satisfying.

I lived in London and the Thames Valley for over 20 years. Any return home for long weekends rest and rehabilitation during this time necessitated an understanding of the cultural differences between the regions, between the pace of life, and between my ears. The looping motorway drive over the tops from Lancaster to Tebay was the final emotional stretch of a marathon drive. I took to stopping at the Cross Keys in Tebay for a large pint of ale. This was intended to wind me down; of course alcohol offers nothing but a false start to relaxation and would serve to wind up instead.

Being based in Cumbria today does not prevent me doing long journeys and I still find the need to pause when coming off the motorway. Now I park the car at the top of the scar and take the short quarter-mile hike up to the Queen Victoria monument. Escapism of the material kind cannot compete with the escapism of nature. This place does. It is easy to bristle with ideas and opinions, to consider a stance to preach, it is easy to kick stones with frustration or applaud hands with joy, it's easy to feel unique - just like everyone else. It's easy to turn over the next piece of life's complex jigsaw on my rock on Orton Scar

The Queen Victoria monument should be recognised as an odd corner suitable for inclusion. With words engraved in granite, and originally filled with lead, the inscription on the monument is severely weather worn. Chris Elphick, clerk to Orton's Parish Council, has deciphered the text as best he can:

> *On the 21st JUNE 1887*
> *This Ancient Beacon was placed here*
> *by the loyal subjects of*
> *Crosby Ravensworth and Orton*
> *to commemorate the jubilee year of the*
> *magnificent reign of her gracious*
> *Majesty Victoria Queen and Empress*

In celebration of the Golden Jubilee of our present monarch, a beacon was lit on 3rd June 2002 and enjoyed, with a firework display, by a good number of local residents. To maintain traditions, the local council has agreed, in principle, that another plaque should be added. I am grateful to Chris for sharing the suggested wording for the new bronze plaque:

On the 3rd June 2002
This ancient beacon was here
erected and lit
by the loyal subjects of Orton
to commemorate the Golden Jubilee
of her gracious Majesty Queen Elizabeth II

The limestone pavements may look bleak as they glint with a wet sheen in the low sun or turn a deep camouflage grey amongst the bracken and heather, yet they can be host to a vast selection of wildlife. Primroses and cowslips pop up from the clusters of moss, sponge and proud grass clinging to the last remnants of earth blown firm into cracked crevice.

Incredible colours can burst through the steel grey from vivid pink herb Robert and even tiny purple orchids. More fantastic names such as hairy rock cress, slender bedstraw and hoary whitlow grass excite the botanist although they may disappoint the ignorant in search of the provocative. Harebells compliment in name the hare population, which I have noticed on the rise since the foot and mouth epidemic in 2001 kept us indoors. The absence of man on the fells for twelve months had disrupted the balance of 'harum scarum' and perhaps helped some native animals claim a larger portion of the grassland. The rabbits still nose over the sheltered outcrops before bounding off white tails bouncing behind. Foxes too survey the land in curiosity and disciplined wariness. If time is to hand, and if not then make it to hand, then simply sit on the stones and watch and listen. Nature will come and after half an hour you will want to stop, or at least slow down, more often.

John Ray laid the foundations of botany and zoology in Britain. He visited Orton Scar during his expedition of 1659. As my botany is clearly lacking I can at least pass on what I have found out about this incredible man. John Ray was the first to use the terms petal and pollen and he was the first botanist to distinguish between monocotyledons and dicotyledons. He was born in 1627 into a deeply political century and one that by today's standards would have sent our fragrant media into a blossoming frenzy.

We will discover more about the birth of the Quaker movement and the activities of Oliver Cromwell soon; remember that the next 50 or so years saw the Civil War, the Plague, the Great Fire and the Botanical Revolution.

Ray studied to become a minister and preached regularly in Cambridge, but the Civil War delayed his ordination. Many churchmen signed a manifesto for reform of the church but in 1662 Charles II demanded every minister to swear an oath in condemnation of reform. Ray would not sign the oath, and subsequently became part of the Great Ejection of 1662 losing his university post, his house and his botanic garden. Ray was left with no income and no place to live.

In his spare time he worked unpaid in the natural sciences and as is seen so often in times of absolute hardship, the genius and commitment of the man prevailed. Beginning with his *Catalogue of Cambridge Plants* in 1660 Ray published highly polished works characterising plants, birds, mammals, fish, and insects. He strived to produce a classification of organisms that would accurately reflect the 'Divine Order of Creation' through Natural Theology. With our (so-called accepted) knowledge today this may not seem controversial, yet at the time theologians spoke that the natural world was a distraction from salvation and must be avoided. John Ray was convinced the Wisdom of God could be understood by studying His creation - the natural world - and wrote:

There is for a free man no occupation more worthy and delightful than to contemplate the beauteous works of nature and honour the infinite wisdom and goodness of God. Let it not suffice to be book-learned, to read what others have written and to take upon trust more falsehood than truth, but let us ourselves examine things as we have opportunity, and converse with Nature as well as with books.

What wise words to contemplate as I sit alone, or with you, if you pass by, atop the scar above Orton. It is difficult not to think of a Creator when sitting up there absorbing the astonishing beauty that surrounds at every degree. My social upbringing certainly bred a 'heart in the country', yet the vast, by far, majority of our population belongs to urban landscape. Do I think of God at times like this simply because of the rock and the view? I have never felt the need to sit in the sanctuary of a church or chapel to experience spirituality. The answer comes quicker when I stop asking the questions too. And I cannot sit on the rock forever.

On the surface, the moor towards Oddendale is very similar to that of Orton Scar and indeed, there is no boundary between the two, yet the Oddendale moor, or Crosby Ravensworth Fell, has proven to be of great attraction to man over the centuries as safe haven and home. Occupational evidence, in the form of collected artifacts and senescent stone circles confirm its seduction to early settlers. Somewhat amusingly Cherry et al in their archaeological survey of 1984 thank the current incumbents for some of their successful dig:

Where the herbage had been particularly well cropped by the sheep, artifacts and potsherds are found lying on the grass, presumably thrown up by mole activity in the past, but where the mole hills have long since eroded away... The difficulty in determining the likely extent of any particular group of artifacts is hardly surprising since we were almost wholly dependent on the random activities of moles and rabbits. Nevertheless, we are likely to have obtained a useful sample of sites, since the drier ground which provides a suitable environment for those burrowing animals would also be favoured by prehistoric man.

The area encircled between Haberwain, Ewe Close, the top of Orton Scar and the motorway has provided plenty of frolicking fun and serious science for our intrigued explorers over the years. The earlier diggers, such as Revd Simpson at the end of the 19th century, may have discovered more media friendly finds (Simpson found remains of burnt bodies) yet today's scrutineers have the advantage of high science. Cherry and his pals took rich pickings in pollen analysis to presume that the moors used to be forested up to a height of 1,200 feet thus deducing that there would be no shortage of wood for building material. Comparison of stone axes and arrowheads appear to confirm a trading economy and community migration between here, Yorkshire and the Lincolnshire Wolds. This is truly fascinating and engaging yet I must admit to losing Cherry when he blossoms into dig-speak when referring to Seal House, a mile to the south of Oddendale:

The lithic assemblage also contains a few non-descript flakes of chert and a flake of volcanic tuft.

Across the moors run a number of ancient highways; somehow at odds to the turnpike that takes the impatient driver off the motorway from Tebay to Appleby, struggling to slow down as he, or she,

maintains motorway momentum and prays that sheep stick still to graze. These ancient roads vary in visibility. The Gallowaygate drove road that took beasts in seven mile stages from here to Low Borrow Bridge, and beyond is more or less the route taken by the returning Scottish Army in 1651 after the defeat of Charles II at Worcester. It is also recorded that Charles II also took the route when on his return from Scotland, making the drove road the M6 of its day. A short distance from the Orton to Shap road, and approachable from routes in and around the Crosby Ravensworth side, is a six foot high monument dedicated to the visit of Charles II. The weather worn inscription gives all the detail we need

although the tale goes that it was a local man named Thwaytes, from Crosby Ravensworth, who was called upon to act as a guide for the source of water and refreshment; this fact is missing from the inscription:

Here at Black Dub, the source of the Lyvennet, Charles II regaled his army on their march from Scotland Aug. 8, A.D. 1651.

Thomas Bland a sculptor of repute and perhaps the Andy Goldsworthy of his time erected the monument in 1843. Bland is also famous for the Garden Sculptures at nearby Reagill and for the carvings on the 23 foot high Victoria Monument at Shap Wells, again only two or three miles distant. The River Lyvennet is one of the few north-draining rivers in Cumbria and empathises with the north flowing Eden by joining it at Temple Sowerby.

It is hard to imagine fell life here some 350 years ago. It is hard to imagine a moor landscape busy with soldiers and horses. It is hard to imagine the day-to-day goings on of an ancient community settled here. Yet this place stirs the imagination. The significance of the 17th century on our region and, as a consequence, our region's significance on the 17th century cannot be overlooked. Those incredibly important radicals of reform are referred to throughout these reams yet I still feel I have underplayed their hand in the social dynamic of the 'north' we see today.

Black Dub is not the only monument on the scar - on the Ordnance Survey maps eagle eyed observers will see Robin Hood's grave marked. It is easier to find on the map than it is on the rolling heather clad moor as one shallow valley merges with another. One would expect to take no belief

in the suggestion made in the name. Perhaps a local hero of similar ilk had a reputation around these parts, particularly when the area was forested. Ironic then that Wainwright's Coast-to-Coast walk passes this cairn to finish at Robin Hood's Bay, Whitby. The aforementioned Sawrey, in his Orton history, offers a link to the 'curious nutting custom' connected to Sherwood Forest's famous rebel. It was considered good luck to load stones on Robin Hood's grave prior to going nutting in local woods, whilst reciting, 'Robin Hood, Robin Hood, here lie thy bones. Load me with nuts as I load thee with stones.' Apparently, in Westmorland at least, Robin Hood is known as the 'Patron of Nutters'.

Above Oddendale is the Hardendale Quarry, an ever-expanding crater that tells me I have gone far enough unless I want to be covered in dust and worse, the fragments of missile thrown forth from heavy haulage trucks rotating with a strength and remorseless vigour matched only by the depth and mass of the quarry itself. Near here is our route back to the Howgill Fells before they disappear over a distancing horizon and we fall into the confederacy of Cumberland.

The B1662 is not glamourous by name yet it is one of the oddest roads in our nation. It takes the careful driver beneath the northbound lane of the M6 to find itself proudly and perhaps a little nervously sitting twixt both carriageways. This short stretch was always a favourite of mine when out with my veterinary father on farm visits. Sat in the front, nose to the windscreen and pre-seatbelt regulation, I could mix dreamlike freedom with that feeling of king of the road, as our movement was independent of the curving snake that had swept across our land. A little bit of territorialism and naîve fear of the unknown would observe huge articulated lorries with huge unarticulated drivers, warrior-like drive over our trenches. Childhood days.

Somehow this little virtual island was detached from the rest of Cumbria. Its unnatural barriers make it feel like genuine no-man's land and the military analogy is all too real. Is it a sanctuary or a prison? This depends on your definition of solitude. Lonely farmhouses glint infrequently over the Shap Fells and, again, make the thoughtful question the definition of lonely. Lonely suggests sad, yet this may not be the case as the occupants have some choice in their solitary existence. It is a great place to think.

SCOUT GREEN, GREENHOLME AND BRETHERDALE

Scout Green, former home of the Scout Green Signal Box, is simply that: former home of the Scout Green Signal Box. Yet its significance as a landmark is second to none in the odd world of the railway enthusiast; obsessives beyond parallel. Harold D. Bowtell in his statistically saturated book *Over Shap to Carlisle* presents detailed descriptions of practically every point and pin along the line, whether removed or still operational. To be truthful it is a delight and like many railway books, is easy to read once you get used to dumping the data. For example, at Scout Green he relates wartime tales of German prisoners-of-war, quartered at Shap Wells Hotel, clambering

into slow moving goods trains to make their, unsuccessful as it turns out, bid for freedom.

Of course, to the railway enthusiast the point of interest would be information regarding the train, its history, where it was built, its speed, its haulage, its driver and much more, rather than details of the escape of Harry Wappler and Heinz Schnabel. As such, much has been written already about the famous trains that have passed along this famous stretch of line. It is hard to pick out individuals, as everyone will have their own favourite.

Many will list 71000 the *Duke of Gloucester*. The history of the train begins in 1911 at Milan University where Arturo Caprotti was challenged to improve the efficiency of the way steam entered and left the cylinders of the steam engine. He completely redesigned the motorcar poppet valve and operating camshaft then scaled the

modification to the much larger steam engine. His pioneering invention still needed work and it this was finally achieved some years later by Great Western engineer Tom Daniels in 1950. Developed in the early 1950s as a replacement for 46202 *Princess Anne*, destroyed in the Harrow Wealdstone crash of October 1952, the opportunity was taken to incorporate the Capriotti and Daniels design features. As such, it was seen as the prototype of the 'next generation' of express passenger steam locomotives. However, as is so often today with true innovation, there was a limited budget for construction costs and a number of corners were cut. These savings dictated a low achievement during service and it was withdrawn in 1962 after only eight years of useful life.

Duke of Gloucester was listed for preservation as part of the National Collection and the locomotive would now be on display in the National

The *Duke* was the chosen locomotive for the inaugural train of the Settle and Carlisle Railway Trust, which ran on 28 May 1991. 1995 saw it cover routes previously barred to steam. On 2 October *Duke of Gloucester* took part in the Shap Trials against the *Duchess of Hamilton* and *Sir Nigel Gressley* and as well as taking the title, it topped the summit at the highest speed ever officially attained with a heavy load. Even then the engine could not fully open out for fear of wheel-slip, as the weather conditions on the day were so (typically) appalling. For the steam-driven statisticians, the firebox temperature reached over 3,000 degrees Fahrenheit during the run with steam temperature at 760 degrees Fahrenheit, burning coal at a rate of 65lbs per mile. It features as one of many 'sporting' and national events where many more people than were actually there claim to have been there to see it. I wasn't but wish I had and now when opportunity arises I make every effort on Steam Days to go and watch these mighty beasts attack Shap Fell. Scout Green is still very popular as a spot for the spotters.

Railway Museum in York had it not been for recognition of its failure. The locomotive's boiler had exhibited mysterious steaming deficiencies at high outputs and with the technicians at a loss to resolve the problem the engine was condemned for scrap. Incredibly this decision was to sew the seeds of a mechanical miracle. In 1973, the 71000 Preservation Society took it upon themselves to rescue the locomotive and their steam driven stamina allowed the formation of the 71000 Duke of Gloucester Steam Locomotive Trust in 1977 and their steam dream really began to take shape. Even then they could not imagine their endeavours would take them beyond their wildest dreams. In 1986, against all possible odds, the *Duke of Gloucester* belched steam again - on the Great Central Railway at Loughbrough - and established a huge reputation for "high speed running and feats of heavy haulage, with steam to spare and power in reserve."

The Advanced Passenger Train (commonly known as APT) was another train sought out for photography and the train spotter's notebook. Development started in the late 1960s with an aim to cut the London Glasgow time to just over four hours and to supersede the Intercity 125 on our electric lines. The APT was given a tilting mechanism to enable negotiation of curves at 30 per cent increase in speed and at the same time increase passenger comfort. During 1982 the APT-P (Prototype) was seen travelling past Scout Green and reportedly reached speeds of 168 miles per hour. At first, passengers felt nauseous because of compensation on the corners yet this was soon resolved. However, the train failed because of those men-in-suits with political agendas and little real thought for the frustrated engineers who after all had succeeded in developing an excellent train.

At the end of July 2003 a Channel Tunnel Eurostar train broke the UK rail speed record reaching 208mph on the first section of the new £1.9bm Channel Tunnel rail link. The Eurostar train broke the old record of 162.2mph set by the Advanced Passenger Train long ago in December 1979. Proving that politics and trains do not mix any plans to run the Eurostar over Shap (and regional use was originally planned) seems to have been forgotten in favour of European commitments.

During the summer of 2003 (14 June) I was delighted to be able to turn my back on the speed up to Shap and take my time enjoying the laid back happenings of the 54th Greenholme Show. Not the easiest place to get to and it is all the better for that, Greenholme sits somewhat stranded above Roundthwaite (itself a 'lost' community) to the south and beneath the road into Shap Wells. Does this make it an island or an oasis? Perhaps

it is a bit of both. The show is a relative baby compared with Shap Show (1861) and Orton Show (1860) yet it still thrives whereas its elder sisters do not.

The show was exactly what I expected and more. Small and compacted into the field above the village hall, a large marquee was host to innumerable competition entries and displays and cakes and teas and everything perfectly rural. The only thing missing were the beasts, a red carded hangover from foot and mouth. There were sports for the kids including traditional egg and spoon and sack and a marvellous relay race round the knolled field. Ice creams were licked, burgers were barbecued and conversations about the old times went on into the late afternoon.

The entrance to Bretherdale is marked by another sheepfold in the Goldsworthy collection. It is easy to miss even though it is right by the side of the lane. First described as 'Two Centuries Fold' because it had been built during December 1999 and January 2000, it was touchingly renamed Megan's Fold after Goldsworthy's regular dry-stone waller Steve Allen's daughter, Megan, who was born on 1 January 2000. This is probably the only significant modernity to Bretherdale.

Bretherdale not only lives in the past, it is the past. Derelict farmhouses litter the valley as if a plague has run through forcing human kind to drop everything and go. Only the beasts remain and somehow, when walking through the valley, the feeling that they now command the fields overwhelms. I am sure it is not just curiosity that makes the cattle and sheep come sniffing and snorting as if to say, 'Who are you and why are you here?' Folk tales report that Bretherdale took

its name from three brothers who lived there some 200 years ago. Records show that the name existed long before this. It is more likely to derive from Brier or Brere.

History is in the making as this prose go to press as plans to construct 27 giant (400 foot high) wind turbines along the Whinash fell above Bretherdale are to-ing and fro-ing between the men-in-suits. Visible for many many miles distant this will without shadow of doubt sabotage the view. Opposition began some time ago to prevent the first 'green' energy option from scarring the 'green' landscape. Some suggest that the sum of around 30 is a deliberate over-estimate to guarantee a minimum goal of 20 or ten or as few as five.

The wind blows in many directions in Cumbria at the moment in the field of wind energy and these giant turbines. Many sites are under review as the Rise of the Machines continues with an unparalleled pace. 'Not in my back yard' is the critics challenge and the subject matter has the potential to make the headlines for the next few decades as man puts survival and disaster alongside with an uneasy passion. Whether to be built or not to be built, the outcome may well become one of our biggest mistakes or one of our biggest successes. Fervent campaigners FELLS (the Friends of Eden, Lakeland and Lunesdale) do their very utmost to protect their vision and secure their own turf. Their efforts should not go unnoticed. Barely ten miles from Whinash sits the Lambrigg Wind Farm, the Trojan Horse of 'only' five turbines for the current furore. Lambrigg is part of our tour and so I will leave the windy statistics until that section later in the book.

Interestingly, this whole area i.e. Borrowdale,

Bretherdale, Orton Fells, Mallerstang and the Northern Howgills were identified in the 1940s as being a landscape of national significance. John Dower, the architect of our National Parks, recommended the designation of the Howgill Fells as a National Park. Later, Sir Arthur Hobhouse, in his recommendation of which areas should be given statutory designation, recognised the value of Dower's analysis of the landscape quality and proposed that the area between the two National Parks of the Lake District and the Yorkshire Dales should be designated as an AONB. Such a designation would have given a clear message to the windfarm developers to look elsewhere but the area, whilst still a proposed AONB, has no such statutory landscape protection because the relevant Government body charged with a duty to so designate i.e. the Countryside Agency, has made no move to take up its 'unfinished business' in Cumbria. Friends of the Lake District and others are urgently pressing for action in this regard.

A feature article in a recent (May 1995) edition of *Cumbria* magazine refers to the days when 20 farmers lived in Bretherdale and only one remains. Mr James Potter had just 'signed up' for Environmentally Sensitive Area status (ESA), a

system that provides incentives for the farmer to take good care of his land and not overstock or allow land quality to suffer. On the face of it, the ESA status is somewhat devalued if some affluent wag can violate the landscape with advowson avarice. The wind farm proposal may yet hold its ground and deliver a metal crop on the top of Bretherdale not because it is a new revolution in energy production but because the faces behind them are veterans of spin.

The true veterans of Bretherdale have all but gone, yet the sheep that have grazed the valley are still there in numbers. In particular the native Rough Fell sheep, little known to the majority of our population but gaining in popularity amongst the sheep fanciers of the world. The Rough Fell is one of the largest carcassed mountain sheep in Britain and adults can weigh on average, up to 54.4kg. Their constitution for long stays on the bleak fells is enhanced by a supreme fleece of white wool, with an average weight of 2.7kg and grade of 32-36. The wool is used for some carpet in Britain but is largely exported for mattress making in France and Italy. Home for the Rough Fell has now extended to Devon as well as Southern Cumbria, West Yorkshire and North Lancashire.

Alerted by the changes inflicted on the farming community by the foot and mouth epidemic two years ago many elder statesmen called a halt to life times of family farming and the sheep stocks on the fells were in turmoil. In promoting the regeneration of fell-life the Rough Fell Sheep Breeders Trust is building a profile and marketability of the Rough Fell so that if such a disaster were to happen again, our agricultural heritage would not be lost forever. With all this in mind, the trust has formed a Rough Fell History Group to make a retrospective and continuing record of everyone involved in the success story that is Rough Fell. They often display sepia tinted pictures of 'how it was' at the agricultural shows throughout the area and are keen to bolster their collection with relevant archive material. They, rather sheepishly, even have badges, posters, stickers and t-shirts to publicise their efforts and

of course, the lovely lamb that is the end product for us all to enjoy.

The Rough Fell is unique and to such an extent that other breeds, and breeders, occasionally display gamesmanship disguised as compliment. For example, a feature that ran in a 1958 edition of the *Dalesman* magazine would still not be out of place today. The article contrasted and qualified the various sheep breeds of our region with typical Yorkshire bravado. Describing the

Swaledale as an 'amazing colonist', the Blackface was dumbed down as 'primarily a breed for the heather hills' and the Herdwick reported to be 'irritable when restricted'. Our Rough Fell was politely portrayed as 'much quieter than the Swaledale, but a bit slower too.'

So, Bretherdale lost and decaying, unsure of its own identity - some would say Lakeland rather than Howgill - isolated between the north-south roads of the M6 and A6, keeps a low silent breath, as fragments of fellside become cornered for development. Local interest in preservation serves to raise the profile too and worryingly this can also result in get-rich-quick idealists jumping on the bandwagon of open space. There is too much at risk here. If I were to shout from the tops that Bretherdale is a lonely silent private valley of extraordinary beauty then it inevitably follows that man will contrive to misunderstand and my compass be contradicted. It is hard not to feel pessimistic about the future of Bretherdale as our precious land is torn apart.

There is a great deal of irony in Megan's Fold signifying the gateway to Bretherdale. Just as timeless Bretherdale becomes an allegory for change so does the sheepfold. John Ruskin, Lakeland orator (who we will meet again in Kirkby Lonsdale) took time from his gothic critiques and gross works of indulgence to pen *Notes on the Construction on Sheepfolds*.

It took me some time to track down a copy of this 1851 pamphlet and I am still not sure if I was disappointed or thrilled to realise that on reading it that it contained not one iota of a clue as to how to build a sheepfold. Neither did it pursue an architectural appreciation of the structure, which

at the very least might have been expected, from the outspoken art critic. The short piece is an exercise in polemical theology with an evangelical bias extending dismay at Romanism and the deepest concerns about public morality. In simple terms, the sheepfold captures the sheep. Whether we can extend the allegory to how we view Goldsworthy's work or perhaps, more profoundly, how we view our potential degradation of our beautiful countryside is open to personal interpretation. Ruskin, over 150 years ago, set the tone in this strange work by stating, and I summarise, that we make elaborate adjustment of tight bandages over our eyes, as preparation for a walk among traps and pitfalls and take daring trustfulness in our own clairvoyance. How right he was.

TEBAY

Some compare Orton and Tebay as you would sisters, one stunningly beautiful, one seriously ugly. This is unfair and untrue. Beauty is in the eye of the beholder and the beautiful woman referred to in the introduction may stimulate virtue in some and may signify vice in others. The danger is in comparison. If I compared Tebay with Tenby and Torbay the reaction may be different to showdown with Tranmere and Tyneside. Tebay should be considered in isolation. In fact isolation is a key word as the coming of the railway isolated workers from Old Tebay by enough feet to build a New Tebay with its railway personality.

The village prospered as a railway settlement and the station, as well as serving two lines, enjoyed a number of sidings themselves complimenting local industry. The metal pegs holding these tracks lent their name to heyday Tebay and it became known across the country as Spike Island. How apt - a ministry morass of migrant metal, magnet to modern movement amid moor and mountain. Traces of the station and sidings are all but gone, the Junction Hotel is closed and the typical terraces on the fell side could easily be mistaken for a mining community were it not for prior knowledge.

The unstretching imagination needed to name the two terrace rows North Terrace and South Terrace is not new to Tebay. Tebay's two distinct suburbs used to be called High End and Low End. The two terraces should not be dismissed as simple railway cottages as their heritage is of great value as is their status on the fell. After all, how many people see these fine architectural parades every day as 'intercity' trains shoot by on the West Coast Line. Twelve stone houses were built in 1862 to make North Terrace and fourteen erected for the south; Whinfell Terrace was constructed in

1898. Length of service was to signify good favour from the railway company and if in that position your house may have been gable fronted.

Any image of the former railway station is locked in the heads of those who lived, worked or passed through Tebay before the station's closure in July 1968. Photographs exist and there are many as Tebay, like Scout Green, was a popular haunt of the enthusiast, yet they can only offer a slim two dimensional teaser of what it must have been like. I have one memory of visiting the station when, around eight years old, I was allowed to run across the passenger bridge and back. Too young to engrain the memory and now I don't know if I remember the occasion or the photographs viewed since.

There are many books and magazines that excel at the railway story and I can only touch the surface here. Better still than the books are the people who were there and still come to visit when steam trains and 'specials' come on excursion. Most of these regulars are happy to be listened to as they project their memories, and steal a few too. Tebay Station is an unusual odd corner because it is no longer there. The community has changed too and having grown quickly because of the railway it must have subsided somewhat when the railway went. A good measure of a thriving community was easily measured by

church attendance. Before the railways, the 1851 return for the Primitive Methodist congregation was only five members. By 1884 Tebay had 81 members and was the strongest of the circuit, and Brough, who did not have the railway, one of the weakest.

Neither Old Tebay nor (New) Tebay sit directly by the Lune and her confluence with the River Birkbeck, down from Greenholme, but prefer higher ground off the flood plain. There was once habitation at this juncture as evidenced by signs of a castle moat; this is now guarded by the loop of the motorway to one side and the rivers to the other. The sunken spirits of the ancient secure site must shudder at the super highway of speed, slalom and stress sitting atop their former stronghold.

With horrors to mind, Tebay's most famous personality is probably the Tebay Witch. Mary Baynes (or Baines, or even Beaynes) was a 'toothless hag' and an 'ugly crone' who survived to the grand age of 90, dying in 1811 from erysipelas (the skin infection that presumably gave her features their reputation.) A number of incidents procured her fame. The first surrounded the death of her black cat. Mauled to death by the dog of Ned Sisson, the landlord of the Cross Keys Inn, Mary agreed to let farmhand Willan bury the loved cat. Willan failed to give the cat a 'proper burial' and she set on a curse on him. Her

reputation began when he blinded himself through an accident with his own farming equipment. She is believed to have taken part in a hunt where she turned herself into a hare and thought to have suffered death at her own hands having eaten some eggs, which she herself had cursed.

Mary's other visionary act was to predict the arrival of horseless carriages at Loups Fell, the land between Tebay and Greenholme. Usually associated with the arrival of the West Coast Line in 1846 it is perhaps yet more sinister to reflect that Loups Fell now houses the intersection where the motorway dramatically cuts across the railway. Anthony Whitehead from Reagill in his *Legends of Westmorland and Other Poems* wrote a dialect poem of some 25 verses about 'The Witch o' Tebay'. My copy of the book is a second reprint from 1952 and it states a first publication of 'about 1856'. The poem is too long to reproduce here but I can give you an excerpt:

> *A fearful teayle I's gawn te tell,*
> *Of wicked deeds by magic spell,*
> *Caused mickle fear, as ye sal hear,*
> *In Tebay Toon lang sen;*
> *Where leeved a hag - an agent she,*
> *To his Satanic Majesty;*
> *As some full weel do ken.*
> *In shap unseemly she was meayde,*
> *Her voice was like the crowken teayde,*
> *Forbidden mien, wi' fiery skin,*

> *Her nwose was sharp, a heuked shap,-*
> *An ower-hang that teuthless gap*
> *Abeune her beardy chin.*

Mary Baynes was an animal lover and, I guess, could not help her looks. Maybe she was a mixture of white witch and black witch (a grey witch?) and as her spirit continues to disturb the occasional guest at the Cross Keys, we should not think too harshly of her. Today, Tebay is more often associated with giving its name to the two Westmorland Service Stations two miles north on the M6. For such a small town, Tebay is perhaps unique for having three service stations nearby, as there is another for long distance motorists just off the motorway slip road and roundabout in Old Tebay.

They are modern day railway stations providing useful employment for locals and benefiting the reputation of Tebay by oft winning 'Best Service

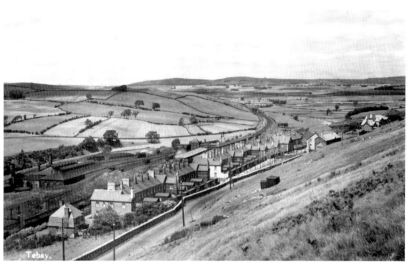

prefer empathetic photographs on the walls to garish advertising and have even been known to place short statements from Indian philosophers on the coffee tables. I will revisit the theme of motorway service stations when we get to Killington further in the book.

If sticking to the smaller roads the route through Tebay is more akin to travelling through the mining and mill towns of the middle-north. Terraces hug the road which itself bends tight to the steep fell and strange cascade of decay amid memory of busier times makes the driver wary to keep hands firm to the wheel and eyes to the road. Even the footpath makes its own higher route to guarantee safety.

Station' awards. Social and culture are not words to feature in isolation when motorway service stations are normally discussed. However, there can be absolutely no doubt that these beasts of our relatively modern society lend themselves to share a unique 'social culture'.

The owners of the Westmorland Service Stations, whilst clearly entrepreneurial, have always recognised the need to alter the attitude of the traveller. With emphasis on the word 'service' these are not 'pit-stops' designed for fast exchange of tea, tobacco and toilet. Their design and atmosphere carefully considers the needs of the motorist and offers restorative calm without making the transition back to motorway too difficult. They

Just past the Cross Keys is the Methodist Church proudly standing with great presence over the railway valley below. Indeed by denominating comparison the Church of St. James, albeit as archaeologically arrogant, stands rather shyly in back street out of sight. I ventured to attend the Methodist Church early in 2003. Not for service but to visit the rear hall for a charity Auction of Promises (the Tebay Auction site!). They were raising money for repair of the leaking roof and as it was torrential with rain outside that night we knew the roof needed repair as it was also raining in the hall.

Like Greenholme Show it was one of those evenings to observe and take part. The flat-capped old men lined the back row ready with nods and winks or simply to make sure they knew what was going on. The women folk busily handed out tea (and biscuits) and the organisers anxiously waited with pens and clipboards as the imported auctioneer (late of Hawes) began proceedings. I spent £72 on a print, thinking it was the original, of the *Duke of Gloucester* attacking Loups Fell. Painted by local man Eric Murphy I did not realise then that I was about to research the *Duke* for this book and the section on Greenholme. I am pleased with my purchase and glad to say that the evening raised £1200 for the roof repairs. I was even happier when I left as I was greeted with recognition as being 'Edgar's lad' and when recalling my late father's veterinary instincts I was then asked by one flat cap if I knew 'owt aboot coos as I av yan needs fettling?'

LOW BORROW BRIDGE AND THE FAIR MILE

From the top of Jeffrey's Mount on one side or Roger Howe on the other, the whole stretch of the motorway twists like a snake across desert sand. Matchbox toys drift along in ceaseless monotony and if the wind is in the right direction the hum can be heard like a persistent drone that will annoy if allowed. When the wind is blowing away the peace on the top is indescribable. Witness the rest of the world going through the motions of everyday living yet at today's reluctant demanding pace, breath calmly, smile and sit with the angels.

The Westmorland Borrowdale tucked beneath Jeffrey's Mount and luring us away from the Lune Gorge provides an alternative and more direct route into Lakeland. The same Friends of the Lake District who purchased Little Asby Common have also added to their bill a portion of land (108 acres) at High Borrowdale midway up this secluded valley. Why it is secluded is left to the historians to debate. Sparsely populated it is deemed to be caught twixt the Howgills and the Lakes yet it is only seven miles long and forms the most distinct conduit between the two fell ranges.

Records suggest that Borrowdale was uninhabited in Roman times when a Roman Fort was in active service at Low Borrow Bridge at the end of the valley. Indeed, it is the fort that gave the valley its name; the 12th century 'Borgherdal' meaning the valley of the fort. There are two farms in the middle of the valley floor only half a mile apart and rather unsurprisingly for an area near Tebay, they are called High Borrowdale and Low Borrowdale. Apparently issues of school catchment areas are not new to these parts. In the 1930s children from High Borrowdale went to school at Selside off the A6 Kendal road, while the children of Low Borrowdale had to journey to Tebay. The companionship of highs and lows is not uncommon as a mile or so over Whinfell Common near Grayrigg are the farms of High Fellgarth and Low Fellgarth, and High Deepslack and Low Deepslack all separated by just a couple of fields.

The valley nearly suffered the same fate as the Haweswater valley by being penned to be dammed and become another

water supply for thirsty urbanites. The social damage may not have been of Mardale proportions, but the ecological picture and geographical framing of the valley would have been unrecognisable from today's dramatic landscape. I would expect that the prospect of Borrowdale Water is now highly unlikely with the Friends of the Lake District at the helm.

A water margin of relief cannot be allowed to flow by without mention of the Three Gorges Dam of the Yangzi River at Yichang in the Hubei Province of China. First imagined in 1919 work has been undertaken on a serious stage since 1993. Only in 2003 did the flooding of the area begin with the planned migration of 1.3 million natives and the loss of 1300 archaeological sites - it seems a high price to pay for the dam's hydropower turbines and their expected creation of as much electricity as 18 nuclear power plants. The sheer scale is within our vision today, yet only 40 years ago our authors were unsure of the capabilities of engineers. Jessica Lofthouse wrote in the mid-1960s of her disbelieving anticipation of the new road through the valley:

How noble they are, the bastions of Howgill, the bald fells of Borrowdale, immortal heights, stronghold of proud Nordic gods. How great the contrasts below, how green the tiny intaken acres belonging to each inch-high farm in the depths of the Lune gorge. A quiet valley, none more so, but along it the new Kendal by-pass is planned. A continuation of the M6 which eventually should carry the motorway not only to Penrith but also on to the Border. That will be the day! When the work begins - the route is already pegged out as I write in autumn '64 - the engineers will have their toughest job yet, making southern stretches of the motorway like cutting cake by comparison. The underlying rocks of this part of Lonsdale are some of the oldest and hardest in the earth's surface.

Jessica Lofthouse, *Countrygoers' North*, 1965 (1968)

The motorway engineers tried to out-engineer the railway navvies with their tarmacadam paintbrush along the Lune Gorge. Qualified master blasters from the gypsum mine at Kirkby Thore (now British PlasterBoard) were hired as explosive experts and the scar lines down the sheer rocks are clearly visible as they now provide rough channels for dripping water off Jeffrey's

Mount as it finds a route to Borrow Beck below. One cannot underestimate the engineering feat of the route masters, some 40 years ago and then a century or so before that when the railway serpent gathered a contour line through the valley.

What of a time before that? The expert eye can see, from Jeffrey's Mount, an old track that dates from Roman times. The route from Low Borrow Bridge, now in the shadow of railway and motorway bridges, took itself down the Lune to Over Borrow, also known as the fort of Galacum, near Kirkby Lonsdale.

Another road, the Gallowaygate, is mentioned in literature of a thousand years ago and was a drove road for taking cattle from Scotland to the Yorkshire markets. Been driven on the hoof the beasts and their charge picked the route off in seven-mile stages and had regular and familiar resting off points at Low Borrow Bridge, Lambrigg Park, Three-mile House, Old Town and Kirkby Lonsdale. The green roads can be seen all around the Howgill Fells and continued to be used even as the new turnpikes opened to improve communications. Of course, the drove routes had the advantage of by-passing villages and especially avoiding the toll-bars.

The antiquarian archaeologist has oft sought delight along the valley floor and the site of a Roman Fort at Low Borrow Bridge has been excavated many times. A Roman bathhouse was found in a dig of 1885 and again in 1951 during a careful study into its role. The luxury lifestyle of bathing was a social pastime albeit steeped in principle and hierarchy. Dry rooms, steam rooms and even whirlpools were all part of the bathhouse and were designed to different temperatures to suit the need. So rooms were kept hot, warm or cold via calculated dispersion of heated air, from water boiled over furnaces, through a hypercourse network of pipes and flues.

Like the farmers of the fells today, the Romans didn't use soap (I am joking about the farmers). Instead they used olive oil (or an equivalent) and a small tool called a strigil. The strigil was used to wipe off the sweat and the oil used for cleansing. The remnant mixture was occasionally bottled from the sweaty bodies of heroes and sold on as a face mask or rub, along with the powers of the icon in question.

Romans would make use of the local terrain for

gardens and ponds (for herbs and fish) and keen-ly honour their heroes once more with statues and ornaments. For longer stays they also planted vineyards and drank wine instead of water, partic-ularly when the water was of dubious purity. It seems that Low Borrow Bridge, whilst one of the earliest forts was simply a staging post and bath-house devoid of vineyards and ornamental gar-dens.

The site is all but invisible today and some would say this a tragedy; others may argue that reburial is a fair status and perhaps more preserv-ing in nature than exposure. Bill Mitchell wrote about the fort in a 1986 edition of *Cumbria - Lake District Life* (September, Vol 36, No 6); he refers to a tombstone that was discovered some 80 years ago by workers digging a culvert for the road. Finding the stone they broke it to use as roofing for their culvert. Past their day the same stones were broken as the culvert was altered into a cat-tle grid. Such is the cycle of material things, mir-roring the life cycles of the very beings that put them there. We cannot preserve everything and this kind of reincarnation, whilst sad in some ways, is refreshing and more natural than we sometimes care to think.

Another interesting find has only come to light recently even though the discovery was made over 150 years ago. Twenty-two coins were bought by James Day, the engineer in charge of the railway construction in the 1840s, from navvies who had found them while working on the line. Day's great-granddaughter nobly handed them over to Penrith Museum a couple of years ago. The set contains coins from the Flavian period (our first century) and helps to confirm that the Low

Borrow Bridge fort was indeed one of the first few forts in Cumbria. It also goes someway to con-firming my suspicions that the Romans were very careless with their money; perhaps mislaid while disrobing for their extensive bathing.

History and fable intertwine once more on the slopes of Blease Fell. Broken Gill wood is affec-tionately known as the heart-shaped wood and is recognised throughout the country by travellers of rail and road. Perfectly situated on the fell it is received with oohs and aahs when glimpsed by merchants of speed in high-speed trains and

touring coaches. These passengers may not know where they are but they will certainly keep their eyes peeled for another snapshot view when next they pass by. The origins of the wood belong to the heart and not the head. Many different tales exist to explain its shape and form. Peter R Williamson, in *From Source to Sea* (2001) nearly convinces with his elaborate explanation of a memorial to railway workers who died while building the railway through the Lune Gorge. Claiming that a tree was planted for each fatality is honourable and could be checked should one be willing to count the trees and compare figures with railwaymen accident documentation. That the wood appears on an early tithe map from 1841, prior to the railway, somewhat diminishes this tale.

I can remember listening with wonder when our geology teacher and competent author, Gordon 'Planky' Wood told us that a pilot from one of the World Wars crashed his aircraft on the fellside and the wood was grown as a memorial. The prevalence of aircraft through the Lune Gorge, particularly a daily run by a noisy Spitfire (I know it is not a Spitfire but I think the pilot thinks so and I don't want to damage his illusion), adds a romantic notion to Mr Wood's explanation. Yet again, the age of the trees defers this story to the wastebasket.

My great-uncle, the late Jim Davidson used to tell of two feuding farming families in the valley that forced two lovers, a son from one family and a daughter from the other, to stay apart. With no future for the affair, the Lunesdale lovers met one last time and in true Romeo and Juliet fashion, he killed her then ended his own life.

Forced together in grief the two families made up their differences and planted the wood in memory of the power of love.

A heartfelt homage comes from Jane Goodwin who wrote to the *Cumberland and Westmorland Herald* in early 2003 with another passed-down tale. This time it was her husband's grandfather Harvey Goodwin who had planted the wood to celebrate his marriage to Ruth Wakefield of Kendal. The detail continues with memories of playing in the bluebell filled wood. Most recently, Hilary Wilson of High Carlingill, has claimed romantic fiction to all the stories and suggested the wood was laid to secure the steep ground, which is prone to landslides. Indeed she points out that the wood is only heart-shaped when viewed from Grayrigg Common as the taller trees to the edges give it this special shape. Close inspection at root level suggests the wood is shaped more like a wedge of cheese. Well, they say cheese stimulates ingenuity though deep dreams and I am sure we can all maintain our favourite tale of love and devotion, with added spice, to pass on to future generations ready to absorb this animated afforestation.

The map of Westmorland in 1974 shows Carling Gill as the boundary between Westmorland and Yorkshire. A logical line headed midway down the Lune Gorge, giving each county half of the valley. The county boundary was moved south with the demise of Cumberland and Westmorland so that Sedbergh could change allegiance and become part of Cumbria. This is not the first time this has happened. How do Sedberghians feel about this? Do they have an identity crisis? It is, I assume, no minor matter.

Just as people are proud to be Yorkshiremen there are equivalent numbers that will be proud not to be Yorkshiremen. The boundary line also competes with that of the Yorkshire Dales National Park and somewhere in there will be a boundary proclaiming the need for a different Member of our European Parliament. The latter line stretches the identity muscles to their extremes but no doubt harmonises a loyalty between Yorkshireman and Westmerian. Only the sheep seem to be uncaring, yet their plight is so often influenced by some covetous convocation on the continent. I raise my hat to the management team behind the Yorkshire Dales National Park, celebrating their 50th anniversary in 2004, for holding firm and enabling part of Cumbria to remain in the Yorkshire Dales. They must recognise this feat themselves as they have themed their anniversary year with the title 'Reaching Out - A National Park for All.'

Colin Speakman, in his excellent book from 1982, *Walking in the Yorkshire Dales*, perfectly describes the division lines when he describes the Yorkshire Dales themselves:

The area does not follow the nonsense of local boundaries that, would you believe it, has half the Howgill Fells in the National Park and half out, that excludes such glorious areas from the park as Mallerstang, Wild Boar Fell, Middleton and Leck Fell, and Upper Nidderdale. Such boundaries are at best an irrelevance, at worst a nuisance.

Mr Speakman goes on to say that it is the people who live in them that decide where they belong. I concur and happily let those who want to say they belong to the Howgills say so and let those who would rather find friend in the Yorkshire Dales or Pennine Range or even Lake Districts Fells do likewise. That said people do make efforts to move to Yorkshire for provocative procreative tourism to ensure that the next gene pool has its passport appropriately stamped.

The narrow lane that clings to the fell almost exactly opposite the M6 motorway is my favourite piece of road in the country. Maybe it is because it reminds me of my youth, maybe because it stands for a past time of a slower pace and a kinder community, or maybe it is simply a very pretty piece of countryside. As a boy growing up in the 1960s this was an open space offering the best playground in the world. The magic of days out and picnics may be romanticised yet one of my proudest moments has been bringing my own children to the same spot, without the history lesson, and letting them enjoy it in exactly the same way I did nearly 40 years ago. Scrambling down to the Lune below and the area we called 'Big Stones' to greet great guffaws as pebbles, and cobbles, and boulders were heaved and pushed and hurled high into the chimerical waters.

Long ago, the naming of Big Stones may have led to its permanent christening as the same simple feeling is endorsed in nearby Far White Stones, Low Park, High House, Hill Top and even Mountain View. My Big Stones was a simple description to confirm the scale of wonder and fun as fell running streams were subject to dam-building and demolition, to forced flood and diversion. We were young engineers imagining Hoover and Aswan, Itaipu and Grand Coulee. And we were getting wet. Then it was time to go home.

The Fair Mile was the first motorway through the Lune Gorge and has often been cross-sectioned to show the Roman input of clay, charcoal and shale. An interesting observation from Macadam (I kid you not) in 1962 was that in dry weather a ribbon of parched brown grass can be seen above a section of the Fair Mile and shows where the memory of the Roman road deviates from the modern tarred road.

The last stage of the wild border includes the crossing of Howgill Fells to the River Lune at Carlingill and Low Borrow Bridge. The fells here consist of the Silurian slaty rocks common in Westmorland, and the scenery differs sharply from that of the limestone. 'Intersecting slopes in angular masses of grey rock, breaking through steep green surfaces, give to this district a very different aspect from the broad swells, rough craggy edges, and brown or purple heath which mark the greater part of the Yorkshire fells'.

William T Palmer, *Odd Corners in the Yorkshire Dales*, 1938

WHITE FELL HEAD

A small stone on the top of White Fell Head marks the place where, in 1998, my father's ashes were cast back to nature. A child of Coppice Howe Farm, Skelsmergh, near Kendal, he studied veterinary medicine at the Royal Dick University in Edinburgh before a 40 year loyal service in practice at Appleby under Graham Holmes. With a natural affinity for beast my Dad was necessarily gregarious with his position amongst Eden folk yet he was also a very private man. In some ways I reflect this mood of scene stealing flanked by a love of loneliness. Struck down at the young age of 72 his remains lie granting him loneliness yet amongst his beloved fell beasts. His passion for tramping fell and dale arise not from a lifetime in field and pasture but from paternal support to the exploring nature of my elder brother during his own late-teen wilderness years and a need for open hill.

With my brother and me flying the nest and exiling ourselves in Edinburgh and London respectively, my father stayed on the hoof with a variety of disparate companions. These companions betrayed his isolation needs, buying into his vanity and came from many walks (sic.) of life. Companions were granted close fellowship and indeed at times were allowed to converse in subjects of their expertise and the merits of their particular views, even if they were wrong. It was always preferable if you came along with some sort of intellect or inquisitiveness, as this would give you the option to learn from his words of wisdom and attention-seeking outspokenness.

Most walkers would be sufficiently entertained to want to come back and in the majority of cases

would be allowed to. He did not distinguish between chosen companions although their physical and mental background would justifiably determine any route planning. All day treks to high peaks were rare if not absent as they satisfied only the energetic with a physical need. My Dad had to link any tour to education.

It's only after death do you realise and make recollective notes of conversations that never found their way to the surface at the time. I have only recently connected this thirst for education and the root of existence (the 'need to know') with my father and the work of his absent uncle, William Hayes. I never talked to my father about my great uncle and it is only now that have I began to research the life and times of Will Hayes.

An inspirited author of some repute, it is with

great comfort that I now find a book written by Will Hayes describing the spiritual source akin to my father's ethic. In *Sweet Calamus* he describes the rare value of reed symbolism. Known to many as sweet flag, calamus may indeed be a simple grass yet it is known to have made an impact on all world religions. For example, the Egyptians conceive of heaven as the field of reeds. The Koran places great importance on writing, and in the first verse of the holy book, reading and writing with the calamus, or reed pen, are praised as the source of all knowledge and all spiritual or scientific paths of change. Christians still celebrate reed festivals and rush-bearings in Lancashire and Cumbria are still common. Calamus is recognised as strengthening incense, helping to build self-confidence and to develop a positive outlook on life.

This is of course one almighty digression from the Howgill Fells, yet it does purvey the spirit of the people. Great Uncle Will lifts my spirits with a cyclical irony combining my personal need to learn and teach, with the discovery that the location of my father's ashes on White Fell Head are identified by a shallow marsh of sedge. One could add that it is no coincidence either that calamus derives from Kalamos, the Greek God who gave his life for his friend at the River Meander; an almost perfect association as the River Lune meanders its way down the valley floor.

But the most precious relic is the story of a hero called Kalamos, the type of the true comrade. Kalamos was the son of the river God, Maiandros (Meander). He was most tenderly attached to Karpos, the son of Zephyr. While bathing one day in the Meander, Karpos was drowned. Kalamos
cursed his father and prayed to Zeus to let him be united to his beloved friend in death. Out of compassion, Zeus changed Kalamos into a reed, and Karpos into the fruit of the field...

The only certain way to World Brotherhood is through the gateway of Knowledge. Education is the secret of progress. Education is light and what the world needs is more light.

Will Hayes, *Sweet Calamus*, 1931

My father introduced me to classical music. As a very young lad I had to like it or lump it as he played to recreational excess as I tried to obtain junior sleep upstairs. Fortunately, I liked it. The Lacrymosa from Berlioz's *Grande Messes des Mortes* derives a magnitude that suits a wallowing landscape combined with speed and freedom. What better melody to bless the air than when driving down the M6 from the Lambrigg and Sedbergh junction into the Lune Gorge? The swirling chorus and sharp orchestra raise the spirit and offer opportunity to fly. It is enough to bring on Faith. On occasion, I cannot help but allow myself this luxurious opera of the senses yet, we should also value silence. Silence is to be treated with respect and understanding its place is a lesson to be repeated.

The Quaker Society of Friends, who hold silence as one of their spiritual ethics were born on these fells. Another appropriate *Messa da Requiem* may be that of Verdi, whose *Libera Me* fades into silence and then it is over. Nothingness. The car may be the vessel for noise while in motion across the dynamic, yet the fell deserves silence. White Fell Head gives silence and nature as one. Then again, there are occasions when I prefer to entertain the mood with

Stevie Ray Vaughan, Lynyrd Skynyrd, even local band, Mrs Knox & the Good Time Boys, and all the Spiritual Cowboys. Music inspires different people in different ways. Oh, the imagination runs wild on these fells.

Writers of prose and poetry, practitioners of craft, design and sculpture, and other art forms all seek and deliver tremendous inspirational works from the rural landscape. Transference of a vision may be the key driver to push their pen to paper, brush to canvas, or finger to clay. I wonder why the composing talents of musically attuned geniuses have not taken inspiration from our fells? I can understand modern music deriving a source from the dramatic immediacy of streetwise urban culture. It truly baffles me why our classical composers have not engaged the spirit of the mountains to a greater degree. To me, their marriage has great potential. Soaring, uplifting, challenging, heaving, enriching, enlightening.

My research to date has given me two examples worthy of mention yet hardly enough to satisfy my curiosity. Alec Hyatt King, in *Mountains, Music, and Musicians, The Musical Quarterly*, October 1945 wrote of the inspiration of the fell scene for composers. He claimed that as nature

clarity of thought and keen composition. Closer to home I do know that in the summer of 1888, Edward Elgar holidayed with his long-standing friend, Dr Charles Buck, at Settle, Yorkshire. And wrote a short piece of music called *Liebesgruss* (Love's Greeting). Less talking and more listening required. I hope I will stimulate readers to share their knowledge of attuned inspiration.

inspired literature in the 19th century, composers wrote musical works using the mountains as a theme. These tended to exploit the local folk tunes and 'different versions of the *Ranz des Vaches*, a type of improvisatory tune played on the alphorn to call the cattle home at the end of the day, were quoted by many composers and served as a model for others desiring to evoke an alpine scene,' The Howgills are hardly Alpine yet it does illustrate the mountain as a model for music. King cites examples in Beethoven's *Symphony No. 6*, Wagner's *Tristan and Isolde*, and Rossini's *William Tell Overture* to silence the popular classical ear.

My second investigation led me back to Berlioz and the Abruzzi Mountains of Italy that lent inspiration for his *Intrata di Rob-Roy MacGregor* and *Harold en Italie*. This is closer to answering my question. His overture is not about the mountain, yet the mountain gave him inspiration to affect

HOLY TRINITY, HOWGILL

The clear grassy way leads to a narrow, metalled lane where you bear right into the hamlet. Here, until 1870, there was a woollen mill that employed many workers. Walk on through the green to Holy Trinity Church, built in 1838. Go inside and enjoy its simple charm. Look in the churchyard for the gravestones of the Herd family. Richard Herd wrote 'Scraps of Poetry', which included a moving poem on a sheepdog helping a shepherd to rescue sheep trapped in snow. Then sit on the seat by the church door and enjoy the delightful scene.

Mary Welch, *Walking the Howgills*, 1998

Today, the tiny hamlet of Howgill may sit with private humility to the rest of the busy world rushing past yet it has been home to one or two idols of the past. Roger Lupton was a native and he went on to become founder of Sedbergh School in the early 16th century and later Provost of Eton.

Richard Herd is buried in the churchyard and although not a household name, he is often quoted as a famous son of Howgill. His contribution certainly befits fifteen minutes of fame in time, but not much more. One of the smallest volumes of poetry likely to found on any shelf, *Scraps of Poetry* contains some 60 poems clearly conceived as a humble wandering shepherd on the fells above. The odd thing about the collection of poems is that they only form the first half of the

book as the second, well the last ten pages, refer to his opinion of the Free Trade Movement of the 1830s.

This may be a simple oddity of feature dictated by notorious publisher and printer Arthur Foster of Kirkby Lonsdale or an insistence of a shared deal by Herd himself who, as you will see below, was gently persuaded to publish his poetry. Going by two titles in the book, one on the contents page and one heading the chapter, Herd's *An Essay on Free Trade* (alternatively titled *Observation on Free Trade*) is dated 5 November 1836. The strength of feeling equates in sympathy to the passionate religious reform seen in the same region in the 17th century.

The issues of Free Trade centred around the Corn Law of 1815, which was conceived at the end of the French Wars to secure the continued profitability of British agriculture. However, it stirred a political debate, which continued until the repeal of the Corn Laws in 1846. The Manchester-based anti-Corn Law League (formed in 1838) provided the crucial opposition to the Corn Laws. Constitutional, social, moral and political issues were at the heart of the league's campaign for a complete repeal of the Corn Laws and not simply aimed at unrestricted free trade (which itself raised the moral problem of trade in slave-produced sugar). Part of the reformist movement, it fashioned ideals which allowed unrestricted economic growth under conditions of free exchange. The Corn Laws repeal is widely accepted as the victory of free trade reform in Britain and marks the advent of the culture of free trade in popular politics.

Feelings were obviously high, even to the point that a humble farmer poet felt strongly enough to position his views. Herd's voice may have been granted the political stage yet the introduction to his *Scraps of Poetry* suggest a more mild mannered man, typical of the local populous.

Some apology for introducing these 'Scraps' to the public may perhaps be deemed necessary. The author is perfectly aware that anyone inclined to criticise may here find ample scope for the exercise of his talents. There are, no doubt, many passages, and many words, which a better scholar might have approved or avoided. Moreover, as nearly the whole was composed while wandering upon the lofty fells of Howgill, without pen or paper, when the ear alone was consulted, and as he does not pretend to be a scholar, under these circumstances it may be hoped, the flow of versification, and the language generally, may prove better than could have reasonably been expected. It may be stated, also, that it is at the earnest solicitation of many author's friends, that he has been induced to permit the publication of these little pieces. To gratify their partial wishes, he has committed his effusion to paper; otherwise they would have remained in the only depository they previously had - the memory.

Richard Herd, *Scraps of Poetry*, Howgill, 1 March 1837

For me, the idolatry fixes on the Postlethwaite family. My granny and grandad were married in this tiny church in 1920 and many of granny's family (the Postlethwaites) also rest their weary bodies in the small graveyard; most notably her closest family of mother and father, Margaret (died 1918, aged 57) and George (died 1927, aged 70).

The Armitstead family, 26 June 1902. Left to right, back - Thomas, John, Elizabeth, George, Anthony. Middle - Jane, Bell, Robert, Elizabeth (née Wharton, born 7 March 1829), Mary-Ellen, Thomas (born 27 February 1825, married Elizabeth Wharton, 26 June 1852), Agnes (married William Hayes in 1887, mother of Hugh Hayes), William. Sitting on floor - Albert and Septimus.

The Parochial Newsletter for July 1920 covers Sedbergh, Cautley (with Dowbiggin), Howgill and others in much the same form as Ewecross Deanery News does today. Indeed, the same surnames abound. Under the Howgill segment is listed the vicar, Rev. W D Auden, church wardens, W Sedgewick, J Fawcett, organist and choirmaster, W Woodhead, and the choir, R Bracken, J Bracken, J Postlethwaite, W Postlethwaite, T Sedgewick, A Airey, N Airey, E Stainton, A Herd, M Herd, L Sedgewick and M Sedgewick. Sunday school teachers are listed as Rev W D Auden, Misses Postlethwaite, A Hird (sic.) and L Sedgewick. The parochial notes headline with church re-decoration and the following paragraph:

Services will be held in the church again on Sunday July 4th. During the time that the church has been closed, the whole of the interior has been re-coloured and decorated. All will agree that the result is good and that Messrs C Bracken and T Sedgewick have done the work well. Then, too, there has been a thorough 'spring-cleaning' by Mrs W Sedgewick and family; no light work when we consider the extra work caused by the re-colouring. The next thing the Church will want will be some new curtains and a new cover for the altar-table at the east end. The new colour will make the old hangings look shabby. The board containing the names of all who served in the war is now in place.

Only one event under births, marriages, deaths is mentioned and that is 'June 3 - Hugh Hayes of Docker, Westmorland, and Frances Postlethwaite of The Ridding, Howgill'. I must assume that they were married in a church in need a lick of paint or one that was closed at the time for redecoration!

For the purposes of research and a personal need to see my living past (this will make sense), in March 2003 I attended a service at Holy Trinity. It was a very wet day, somehow appropriate for the beginning of Lent and the Rev. Anne Pitt's sermon relating Noah's tale to Baptism. Our first hymn was *Forty Days and Forty Nights*. I later learned that the congregation of fourteen was larger than usual. Expecting the elderly to be in main attendance it was strangely refreshing to find three children amongst them. The flood story related well not only to the weather of the day but of an experience of the church from the last century. A high flood ravished the walls and banks between the beck and church and took no mercy on the graves that were at beck side.

As the service proceeded in moments of silence all I could hear was the gentle rush of Howgill Beck by the church. The continuity of prayer was still there analogous to the continuity of the waters as it was within local recall, and before that to the first days of the church in 1838 and to its predecessor the old chapel dating from 1685 on the other side of the beck. My hybrid cross-link to the continuity is through the Postlethwaites of Ridding. The distinction of location being necessary as there are Postlethwaites at nearby Crosedale. Inevitably the two strains will be related if the genetic hierarchy were investigated.

As we know, Frances Postlethwaite (date of birth - January 1890) married Hugh Hayes on 3 June 1920 at Holy Trinity. Hugh, one of three brothers was born in July 1892, and, with elder brothers Thomas (born June 1888) and Will (born January 1890), belonged to Hollins Farm a mile south of Grayrigg. Their father was William Hayes (1842-1897) and mother, Agnes (1853-1927), who was an Armitstead. Locals will tell you that there are plenty of Armitsteads, as there are Postlethwaites still living and thriving I hope, in the area. Agnes came from Aikrigg above Killington; a farm with one of the best, and rarely observed, southern aspects of the Howgills and

Lune Gorge. Agnes was one of thirteen children of Thomas Armitstead (born 1825) and Elizabeth Wharton (born 1829). Elizabeth belonged to the Whartons of Sunbeggin (sic.) and her father Lancelot (born 1794) had direct lineage to Sir Thomas Wharton (1495-1568) of Wharton Hall and Mallerstang Forest.

This elongated family tree serves not only to confuse but also to confirm the matrix of kin across the region. Lancelot's grandfather, for example, married Isobel Whitehead (at Orton on 1 August 1753) who was daughter of John Whitehead out of Raisbeck and no doubt of lineage to Quaker George Whitehead. Thomas Armitstead and Elizabeth Wharton were married in 1852; the Armitsteads regrouped on 20 June 1902 for a Golden Wedding family portrait (see picture). There is clearly a mustached similarity between the menfolk, whether the trend is continued in such style by my brother and me is open to debate. To bring close family up to date, Will Hayes went off to pursue spiritual matters (marrying Dorothy Manners daughter of popular artist William Manners), Thomas farmed at Bankhouse near Patton and Hugh, my grandad, took Frances off to Coppice Howe Farm at Selside. My father and his brothers Hugh and Albert, and sister Phyllis were brought up at Coppice Howe. And so I return to Howgill and Holy Trinity and a community that shares my blood. Or rather, I share theirs.

The gravestones of Holy Trinity tell the story of the compact community. There are very few different surnames. The same names live in the area today. My second cousins, both of octogenarian outlook were at that Lent Service in March - Fred

Yew Trees. Brimble makes a more fragrant association between the yew and death in *Trees in Britain* (1948) by assigning the protective nature not to the church but to the fact that the yew was the most common wood used for making the weapon of the day, the long-bow. These Howgill yews are well groomed and cared for.

We can expect the same treatment of the new tree, not a yew tree, a foot or so outside the school hall, on the bank above the church. Howgill's Millennium Oak, planted and established in 2002, has some way to go before it reaches

and Peggy welcomed me with a warmth and mutual pride. The organist is Freda Trott herself an octogenarian and well known by many as author of times past and present around Sedbergh and Howgill.

While looking at the church and its very special location, it is impossible not to admire the yew trees that guard the gate. Somewhat sombre, sometime sinister, although that impression may be governed by its typical location of the grave-yard, the yew is a testament to the timelessness of churchyards and cemeteries. Ken Mills in his *Cumbrian Yew Book* (1999) relates an early reli-gious reference made by Quaker Founder George Fox when he sought the largest yew (of Lorton Vale on the River Cocker) in order to speak to a crowd of Seekers. Fox, clearly a visionary and an early marketing man no doubt, chose the site to preach fully aware of the spiritual undertone. Wordsworth also found that yew an inspiration in

the height and girth of the other trees around. I am sure it will, as the care and devotion in the community is very special indeed. A plaque in the wall highlights the corner of the gravel car park where the oak can be admired. How nice it will be to visit every year and watch it grow.

I get a feeling of comfort when entering Howgill. This may be an instinctive 'coming home' emotion, grasping at roots. Whatever it is, comfort is made easier by the recognition of the community that is the 'Dales Village'. A small selection of houses and steadings clustered down shallow banks by a beck create a perfect picture, a picture of perfection. Unlike some larger vil-lages Howgill does not have a shop or a post office or a pub. It did have a mill. The corn mill would have been as essential to the community as the church or my latter list. It is some measure of the erosion of village life that the shop, the post office, the pub are also slowly (some would say quickly) disappearing from the village of any location.

The mill at Howgill was clearly a grand affair with buildings at both sides of the river. Apart from a cluster of stone slabs and foundations only the Mill House remains intact, as a private residential property. The water corn mills were prevalent throughout the Dales utilising to maximum effect the water rushing from the high fell. The mill owners would take a permanent right to the water and successful businesses were born.

The inevitable pattern of global trading, seen today in any new market, ruined the local mill as cheaper imported corn led to a growth of steam mills at ports. By the 1880s the Cumbrian windmill and watermill era was over, unable to compete with the coastal steam giants at Barrow, Carlisle, Silloth and Whitehaven. Some mill owners were able to adapt to textiles, again this was short-lived because of the same global economics. Mill relics are dotted all over this party of our countryside. Birks Mill at Sedbergh has that air of sweat and dust as the ravined Rawthey rushes by; then more mills defend their derelict corners further round at the appropriately named Millthrop, along the Clough in Garsdale and down the Dee in Dentdale.

Today, working watermills are practically non-existent with the exception of working re-enactments in living museums. The Water Resources Act of 1963 was a body blow to Cumbrian mills as the local body were given the authority to enforce the Act according to their own interpretation. The northern region took on board the small print where 'an owner of a waterwheel or turbine must declare how many thousands of litres of water will be consumed each year.' A heavy levy was incurred on the same. However, no-one seemed to realise that such mills do not actually 'consume' any water at all; all their water being returned to the river. The legislation even ignored the practical input that the mill owners made to maintaining weirs and improving fish-runs. Such short-term economies truly ended the era, although many mills in the region had gone long before this maladministration. It is a shame because it allows me no space to expand on the industry and to introduce lovely mill terms such as flaunch, rim, vanes and gudgeons, launders, klews, brace-rods and undershot felloes. A time long gone.

The intensely rural quality of Westmorland penetrates this corner, the border line of Yorkshire. You feel it in the sunken village of Howgill and the common land beyond it where butterworts and forget-me-nots brighten the boggy patches, but chiefly round the farms, whose methods are often those of the other county. It is evident in the hedging and walling competition held in February. The fact that these two arts could be carried on close to each other shows the mixture of upland and lowland; at one time there were sections for ploughing, but there are no arable lands here now.

Ella Pontefract & Marie Hartley, *Yorkshire Tour*, 1939

CROOK OF LUNE AND LOWGILL

Not to be confused with Crook o' Lune closer to the coast, the Crook of Lune Bridge is my favourite of all the Lune bridges. Its height and span gracefully offer protection and distance from the river below and its tightest of narrow gaps wrap around the passing car providing a guarding insulation to fulfil the security. How can such a fragile looking structure proffer such power? How can such an ancient crossing retain its strength? Yes, this is a favourite odd corner, where I challenge anyone not to breath in when driving across the bridge, where you want to have another ride over except suitable turning points fail to appear and you cannot turn back, where you are certain magic and fable and mystery live, and where dizzying emotions of fear and attraction combine to confuse and entice.

E. Jervoise in his lovely book *Ancient Bridges of the North of England* (1931) calls it 'most attractive' and adds the statistics to confirm its mysticism. With two segmental arches, each spanning a distance of 32 yards, the width

between parapets is slightly less than seven feet. Records show repairs to the bridge in 1702, 1758 and again in 1817. I do hope someone is looking after it today; even on these quiet back roads the traffic is heavier than it once was. Yet, perhaps the bridge knows best; it still seems comfortable with the heavy Lune waters, pictured during the 2004 floods.

This corner of the Howgills gives an emotional feeling of what the Lune is all about. They say the name Lune is derived from a reference to white stone although there must be some inspiration from lunar inference, the moon, our orbiting satellite that has such a pull on Earth's ocean and our tolerance of mood. Attracting the loon, the lunatic and the loner perhaps? What would Freud, Jung and Kant make of the individual who finds comfort sitting alone by this river? Then again, the Lune is well known for attracting that strange beast, the fisherman.

I tried fishing as a youngster and did not take to the hobby as much as my mates did. Yet it was still more common amongst us 30 years ago than it is today. Many do take up rod and line but many have their hobbies spoon-fed them by the marketers of corporate greed feeding habits of addiction and craze. Still, some may debate that fishing is an addiction and, forgive the pun, once bitten, it may be difficult to resist. As then, I have no need for damsel nymphs and little black dries today. The Lune is recognised as a river that played host not only to the fisherman of hobby but the fisherman of need, the poacher. Fishing, like all specialist sports, likes to

LOWGILL, NR. SEDBERGH.

embrace its own terminology and in researching the poacher I learned that he would use tools such as a gaff, click-hook and lister. My research even led to me to hear that mucking out shovels were used to thwack the rising salmon over the head.

Folk-lore inspired by a true event makes me recollect an incident from only this year when walking the Lune above Devil's Bridge near Kirkby Lonsdale as a guide to two lady friends, we'll call them Sharon and Janet, when we saw a man firing small stones in the river with a catapult. I made up a tale that it was not the fishing season and he was trying to hit a salmon. Maybe Sharon was correct after all to believe my fishing tale, for all I know now about the techniques of poaching it may indeed have been true.

The fisherman is far from immune from today's troubles as he contemplates a solitary existence on the banks of the Lune. Fishing diseases go in cycles, as do the population cycles of the fish themselves. Forty years ago the unpleasant disease ulcerative dermatic necrosis (UDN), portrayed by the appearance of white patches across the fish scales, devastated fish numbers. Today, stocking is carefully controlled and monitored by the various angling associations as they stoutly protect their turf. Even they have new hurdles to deal with. The outcome of foot and mouth saw many gallons of treated detergent drained into the river network. The damage has not been direct to

the fish stocks, yet it has destroyed the caddis fly found in the becks. As a result the fish that feed on the caddis have had a crisis and the food cycle is broken. Many angling societies worry about the amount of sheep dip that finds its way into the rivers and the unknown damage that it is causing to the food chain. The fisherman has plenty to think about.

Eleven Arches, Lowgill.

I enjoyed my dip into the fisherman's sack and next year will make an effort to observe the daytime surface activity of the medium olive in June and the large dark olive in September. If my interest continues I will seek out the upwinged iron blue dun and the small spurwing. In truth my only similarity with the fisherman will be the love of water and a great fondness for the Lune.

The food chain does not stop at the fish. They are prey too. Thankfully a combined survey by the Environment Agency, Wildlife Trust and English Nature has declared a 20 per cent increase in numbers of otters throughout Cumbria over the last decade or so. The 1960s proved hazardous for the otters as well as the fish population due to the harm caused by toxic pesticides. Shy and nocturnal, it is a wonderful sight to see an otter in 'performance' and good news that they are back. Conservationists and the water companies themselves have embarked on a clearer aim to bring river life back to nature and must be congratulated. Otters have been protected, since 1981, by the Wildlife and Countryside Act such that they cannot be killed, kept or sold without a licence. The licensing extends to the dealing in stuffed otters too!

The food chain spreads it wings further as otters are also known to feed on coots and moorhens. Gastronomic otters occasionally favour frog over fish. Whilst there may be keenness to otter spot, the sight of a cormorant is less popular. A cormorant controversy is expanding as fast as their population devours the inland fish stock. It is presumed in some quarters that man's hoovering of the ocean has forced the cormorant inland to feed. A simple observation is made more complex by the distinction of two breeds of cormorant identical to the casual observer. *Phalacrocorax carbo carbo* is primarily a marine species, breeding on rocky coasts from northwest France through the UK to northern Norway. Quite distinct from this is *Phalacrocorax carbo sinensis*, which inhabits mainly freshwater and nests in trees and unlike its

cousin, is concentrated in the western Baltic and central Europe eastwards as far as China and Japan. Both are protected under the Wildlife and Countryside Act of 1981 and the broader European Directive on the Conservation of Wild Birds, 1979.

The angler does not want to distinguish between the two cormorants and does not need to know which is eating 'his fish'. The angler wants to control the cormorant and it has reached the point in population demographics that organised culling is being proposed. Needless to say, the riverbank has two sides and an agreed strategy is some way off. Many people say that the fishing birds, herons and grebes, regarded the same as coots, waterhens, kingfishers and swans, and accepted as part of the natural aquatic environment and as such adding to the pleasure of angling, should be placed alongside the cormorant as a threat to fish stocks. I expect future legislation will dictate how the angler is supposed to behave. We will cross the bridge of how he actually behaves when we come to it.

The most striking view from the Crook of Lune

Bridge is another bridge and one that most people will be familiar with, although not from the lower angle. Lowgill Viaduct is a landmark for users of both the M6 and the west coast railway line. Eyed to the left, it is the last snapshot vision before road and rails veer out of the Lune Gorge and head towards the exit gates of Cumbria. Lowgill Viaduct is often called Beckfoot Viaduct and was opened in 1861. To be precise and once more satisfy the statisticians in the sidings, the line was opened on 24 August 1861 to goods traffic and on 16 September 1861 to passengers. The closure to regular passengers came as long ago as 1 February 1954 (a sad 50th anniversary in 2004) and finally on 1 October 1964.

The 'little' North Western Railway from Lowgill to Sedbergh to Barbon to Kirkby Lonsdale to Ingleton to Clapham was a useful west coast diversionary route during these, its latter extended life. Goods closure inevitably came on 7 December 1964 even though a few sneaked their way through until 26 July 1966. Players of statistics may furrow their brows and query my epoch-like quotations from the aforementioned Harold D. Bowtell and will delve deep into their own archives to contrast and contest. What of Broughton and Harris in *British Railways Past and Present* Number 1 Cumbria who give 1 March 1965 for the last goods effort on its way to the depot at Ingleton? If facts and figures flick your switch then you will enjoy the fact that the rail journey from Carlisle to Leeds via Lowgill and Clapham Junction is about two miles less distant than the route employed today via Appleby and Settle.

Driving out of Beckfoot there is a small side road signposted Lowgill and a diversion that may feel like an invasion of privacy. At the end of this lane, as well as an alternate view of the viaduct are the residential properties that once accompanied Lowgill Railway Station. Closed, according to Bowtell, on 7 March 1960 the station remains

have long gone, as has the track (lifted in 1967 according to Broughton and Harris). The station house and short row of railway houses that remain are beyond adequate description sitting as they do, far removed from any other property with the best views in the country across to the Howgills and down to Firbank, and prey only to the whirr, whiz and whoosh of passing intercity trains and the drone, drone, drone of the motorway barely 400 yards away.

The potential for rebirth of this interesting railway line is not beyond the realms of fantasy for this off shoot from the West Coast route at Lowgill. The whole route would make a superb footpath too, but the land now belongs to farmers and landowners in segments and the only 'beast' allowed to travel the line have four legs or wings. With a veterinary father, as an accompanied child I was occasionally availed of certain land access rights and with farmer's permission I remember walking across the viaduct in my younger days. Like the line itself, this is a very distant memory and not likely to return for a very long time.

FOX'S PULPIT, FIRBANK

Some have suggested that George Fox knew perfectly well there was a great people to be gathered; they were the Westmorland Seekers, whose little groups were springing up in a rudimentary organisation all over Westmorland and North Lancashire and the Yorkshire Border... The message preached by George Fox on Firbank Fell was the very one the Seekers were looking for... 'The Kingdom of Heaven did gather us, and catch us all, as in a net,' wrote Francis Howgill, 'and His heavenly power at one time drew many hundreds to land, that we came to a place to stand in and to wait in, and the Lord appeared daily to us, to our astonishment, amazement and great admiration... Francis Howgill was arrested in Kendal Market in 1663 and tendered the Oath of Allegiance, which he refused to take. On his second refusal at Appleby Assizes, he was praemunired and committed to Appleby gaol, where he died in 1668.

Elfrida Vipont, *George Fox and the Valiant Sixty*, 1975

High on Firbank Fell around 100 yards from the narrow road that leads from the redundant Black Horse on the Sedbergh to Kendal road north across to the Tebay to Grayrigg road sits a metal plaque in the rocky outcrop. The route to the rock is unmarked and the plaque is simplicity itself. No tourist accessories are to be found and the only people seeking this site will have an understanding of those first Westmorland Seekers who crowded on this fellside 350 years ago.

George Fox came into Westmorland and the

Yorkshire Dales on a spiritual mission. George Fox was a charismatic visionary, with, allegedly, well-developed psychic powers. Twentieth century Quaker Rufus Jones was to write at length about the mysticism of new religions. Not to be misunderstood as sinister or supernatural as with magic or, in the extreme, voodoo, it is a generated feeling of shared peace, calm and knowledge of love. That image of calm is disturbed by some recollections. According to George Fox's journal, 'Justice Bennett was the first that called us Quakers because we did bid him tremble at the word of the Lord. This was in 1650.' They have also been known as 'Tremblers' and it is easy to see how potent a body they were set to become. They should, however, not be confused with the Shakers who hail from Manchester.

After touring the lowlands below, staying the night at Briggflatts Farm the home of Richard Robinson, Fox was persuaded by Francis Howgill to talk at a meeting at Firbank. The chapel of Firbank was also on the hill, only a fragment of the churchyard now remains as it was damaged by a storm and fell into decay. Fox perhaps swayed by the numbers who had heard of his preaching or perhaps by impulse of intuition, spoke outside the chapel from a rock above the expectant crowd. He was later to have said that it was important to preach outdoors to fully give the understanding that the chapel was a mere house and that God could be found on the mountainside as much as in the holy building. The plaque describes that day:

Let Your Lives Speak. Here or near this rock George Fox preached to about one thousand seekers for three hours on Sunday June 13, 1652. Great power inspired his message and the meeting proved of first importance in gathering the Society of Friends known as Quakers. Many men and women convinced of the truth on this fell and in other parts of the Northern Counties went forth through the land and over the seas with the living word of the Lord enduring great hardships and winning multitudes to Christ.

There is little room to park a car in the lane leading to the rock; maybe room for two and at a squeeze three. The farm animals of the fells use the small square of land in front of the rock; a pile of fodder surrounded by heavy hoof prints is not uncommon. The grassy banks that surround the outcrop are notoriously waterlogged; even the right of way off the fell over Hill Top Heights and Master Knott provides a course for water. This land offers physical humility to that time centuries ago, as does the people that took away a belief of truth and peace and silence and equality.

George Fox, and later William Penn, and most recently men like Rufus Jones have influenced Quakers in America and many Friends now come on spiritual homecoming visits to see Fox's Pulpit, Briggflatts, nearby Swarthmoor and the Northern Meeting Houses. Are they tourists too? Perhaps by one definition, yet I do feel they have a simple right to witness their roots. They come on a spiritual pilgrimage and, I hope, exhibit the principles of peace. These spiritual tourists may be a million miles away from the combated American tourist 'serving' his country in the Middle East and elsewhere.

One cannot deny the 'success' of the Society of Friends. Especially as it was such a difficult start

for them as they held views considered anti-establishment and led to many years of persecution as heretics and a threat to orthodoxy. Of course, they were not unique as a group 'seeking' a rediscovery of Christian faith. The Wesley campaign was only around the corner, and many more sub-sects of variations of challenging faiths based on core values with local interpretation. Indeed, not too far down the road, at Warrington there was a group of Congregationalists called the Methodist Quakers. Cynics view the modern American Culture of Free Church with heightened ridicule yet it is simply an extension of the northwest region's religious evolutions - the spiritual revolution - of Fox, Wesley et al.

The first Quakers to land in America were two women, Mary Fisher and Ann Austin, who made their way there as early as 1656. The pluralism of metaphysical theory, distinct from the exclusivist ideal, makes for an engaging journey. Even today, with the benefit of internet, our past and our very small world can be opened in front of our eyes with a touch of a button. "The Plain People" is a term used, with common consent to the denominations of Lancaster County, Pennsylvania, which incorporates, amongst others the Mennonites, the Amish, the Church of the Brethren (often called Dunkards or Dunkers), the Brethren in Christ (River Brethren), the United Zion's Children (Brinserites), the Yorkers, the New Mennonites or Reformed Mennonites.

How far removed are these sects from the 199 sects listed in the 1646 *Gangraena* volume by Presbyterian Thomas Edwards, which listed our Quakers with Seekers and Ranters but also Mugletonians, Familists, Diggers, Fifth

Monarchists, and Grindeltonians? George Fox was to develop his denomination on the theory of Apostasy.

My Great Uncle Will was a pacifist yet not a Quaker as he extended his personal understanding of interfaith by accepting the Free Religious Movement and Unitarianism theories. Whilst leading the Order of Great Companions from his new church at Hertha's Chapel, Meopham Green in Kent, he still pursued an allegiance with the Quaker Movement to write a biography of Francis Howgill. This was clearly borne out of a geographical tug as Francis Howgill was brought up at Todthorne, now barely a ruin, next to Kiln Head Farm, and but a stone's throw from the Hayes' farms of Hollins and Thackmoorhead. Will Hayes acquired the latter farm, sometimes referred to as Thatchmoor Head, with the intention of making it a 'Rest Home for Pilgrims on their way to Firbank Fell'. It was inevitable that Will Hayes as an author would write about Francis Howgill, just as it is inevitable that I find myself writing about Will Hayes.

Francis Howgill was born in 1618 (six years before George Fox) in a farming community yet he took up the trade of a tailor. A serious minded man known to feel a religious depression in trying to find out which of the dissenting denominations would satisfy his thirst, the Westmorland Seekers had sung the right tune. When he heard Fox preach at Firbank Fell he found that the Quaker message qualified his thoughts even further. Companion to Edward Burrough working in London under the guise of attending threshing and harvesting meetings, they became responsible for establishing Quakerism. Howgill made many

a direct approach to Oliver Cromwell and the dramatic history of this century carried the influence of his actions across England and even throughout Ireland. Francis Howgill died a prisoner in Appleby gaol and only then did he return to the Howgills where he was buried in an unmarked Quaker grave at Sunnybank Farm just outside Grayrigg.

The story of Firbank Fell has often been written. The fell is a place of Pilgrimage for Quakers. In 1924, on the occasion of the tercentenary of the birth of George Fox, 300 Quakers from all over the world gathered on Firbank Fell and held a meeting there. I was present at that meeting and spoke. I told the assembled Quakers that Firbank Fell had been part of my playground as a boy (for I had lived in the valley below). I had stood on George Fox's Rock Pulpit and given imaginary addresses to my two brothers! Then I told them something of what the story of Francis Howgill had meant to me, and how it had taken me out of the Dales - to prison and to another pulpit to preach Peace and Universal Religion.

Will Hayes, *Gray Ridge - The Book of Francis Howgill*, 1942

GRAYRIGG

The Church of St. John the Evangelist dominates the grey skyline and everything about Grayrigg. From a distance you might mistake Grayrigg for Orton, excepting on closer inspection its only similarity is the climate. The triangular ecclesiastical parish of Grayrigg heads north as far as Huck's Bridge on the A6 to Shap Summit, to Lambrigg and Docker to the south and across to Dillicar Common to the east. The driver may not see Grayrigg as sitting on a ridge that gives it its name. The rambler investigating the fields and tracks around will certainly recognise a ridge and the lofty top that is home to the church, school, village hall and a cluster of tidy homes.

The Romans and then the Saxons were in evidence in Grayrigg during the first part of the first century, yet it was not until the Danes rampaged across Cumbria in 832 that 'Gray Ridge' derived its name. It is of interest to note that cartographers and linguistics took to amending Gray Ridge to Grayrigg (and Lamb Ridge to Lambrigg) whereas Bridge in village names deferred in the other direction from Brigg, e.g. Patton Bridge, Garnett Bridge. It is presumed that the nickname for badgers of 'greys' gives the name to Grayrigg as the area is well known as a sett community. Just as nearby Brockholes farm in Low Borrow Bridge (and Brockhole at Windermere) takes advantage of the 'brock' alternative.

Badgers do not have an easy life even though they are protected. As sometime carriers of bovine tuberculosis they are often linked to transmission of the bacterium to cattle, making farmers wary of their activities. Even as one of Britain's best-loved wild animals, badgers are still threatened by vigilante pest-controllers and in particular the inhumane activities of badger baiters. Against the law since 1835, badger baiting is amazingly on the increase again as those who carry their heads on their shoulders simply to hold their hats struggle for entertainment.

Our Cumbrian badger population regularly set the headlines with our farmers struggling to cope with a confused message from central government. Bovine tuberculosis is an awful disease that, in 2003, affected 5500 farms, with 6% of the country's 95,000 herds infected. Cumbria is less affected than other parts of England (fourteen farms infected in late 2003), yet when they hear

words like 'epidemic' and phrases like 'waiting for scientific evidence' our farmers are understandably anxious. No doubt the badgers aren't happy about it either.

The Greys around Grayrigg may fair better yet they are still seen lifeless by the verge of the narrow lanes as over keen motorists prefer speed to safety. With transport in mind it is worthy to comment that badger is slang for the itinerant tinkers and hawkers who travelled around selling goods from horseback along the packhorse routes and green roads.

With Quaker Francis Howgill as Grayrigg's most famous son, author John Punshon was probably unknowingly apt when he related the colour in the title of his book on the short history of the Quakers based on their humility of dress, *Portrait in Grey* (1984).

For a small community Grayrigg's history is fairly well documented. Records show that a corn mill was built here in 1274 and John Somervell, author of the excellent tome *Waterpower Mills of South Westmorland* considers the original mill to have been on the site of the present High Mill in Grayrigg. Somervell also places mills at nearby Lambrigg, Firbank, Patton and Whinfell, stating, 'It is a surprise to find so many traces of mills in such sparsely populated districts as Grayrigg and Patton and one can only conclude that in the past the population was much greater.'

I have walked the criss-cross network of field paths in the area and, population demographics or not, I do know that there are plenty of springs and waterways on shallow hills to make many small mills a possibility. Half a mile from the church at Grayrigg below Grayrigg Hall Farm, at the turning over the small bridge, is a delightful spring rising out of a shallow basin beneath a tree. It has served me well with refreshment when my knapsack bottle has run dry.

Grayrigg seems to be able to get water from below and plenty from above too. On a recent visit, I chanced to look around St. John's and was welcomed by priest-in-charge, Revd Brian Pedder. He was concerned about the state of his south wall as it was deteriorating in ability to keep out the persistent rain so familiar to Grayriggians. Indeed, just as the British are so fond of discussing matters climatic, the people from Grayrigg have a minor obsession about their rainfall. And with good cause.

The parish magazine, *The Grapevine*, religiously

a healthy size and is clearly in loving care.

In thoughtful mind I resisted the temptation to suggest that Revd Brian should contact the people responsible for waterproofing Smardale Viaduct in case he was still sore at the railways for closing Grayrigg Station. On reconsideration I doubt if he would be bitter, being a member of the cloth and for the fact that the station closed its doors way back on 1 February 1954. In full Grayriggian statistical mode I should add that the Grayrigg signal box, opened in 1926 and closed in April 1973 making way for power signalling. There is barely a trace of the station today. The modifications for high-speed travel continue and only recently the railway companies fenced off an

gives detailed measurements of their exceptional precipitation. From February 2003, 'February had a rainfall of 85.8 mm (3.38 inches). The average for the last 11 years being 155.4 mm (6.12 inches). At the same time last year it was 313.3 mm (12.33 inches).' London's rainfall for February over the last three decades averages a meagre level of around 35 mm.

Grayrigg has had a chapel on the site of the present incumbent since 'shortly before 1469', this is how the parish notes describe the history. The chapel was rebuilt in 1708 and again in 1837 when it had 420 sittings of which 120 were galleried. The gallery was removed at the beginning of the 20th century yet the building still commands

old footpath over the railway (above Beckhouses) where the Dales Way used to cross the line. With money and gallant action they have built high standard stiles, gates and steps providing a short detour and alternative route for a few hundred yards.

Such contribution would probably not mean much to our reverend's waterproofing needs and he will not have a budget like the corporate railway. Church life seems analogous to farm life. The richer churches prosper, as do the high-ranking farms, while the poorer churches will always struggle against poverty in similar manner to poorer farms. I do not know what Revd Pedder puts in his pocket at the end of his financial year, nor do I want to, yet the records for the past prove interesting and, yes, statistical reading. In 1366, the priest's salary was £4 a year. Ten years later it was increased to £5-6s-8d (£5.32p) per year. The agricultural relationship was more poignant then as the priest would usually be part-time farmer and part-time parson, needing both occu-

pations to maintain a living.

Westmorland's second town, Kendal, influences Grayrigg and the hamlets around as the fell-line behind protects them from the likes of Sedbergh, Tebay and Shap. This was very much the case 300 years ago when John Wesley visited and left on each occasion not best pleased with the local attitude. In 1753 Wesley wrote, 'I was a little disgusted at their manner of coming in and sitting down without any pretence to any previous prayer or ejaculation.' Somewhat dejected his later writings almost despairingly said, 'I once more cast my bread upon the waters and left the rest to God.'

It took a century before the chapel life really took to thriving, perhaps when the word from the eastern Howgills and Dales had finally got over the Dillicar high-ridge. Today, many have slumped secularly as faith tends towards television rather than community; the Primitive Methodist's Chapel of 1903 above Whinfell Tarn being a good example. St. John's still commands fine attention. While it was being built in 1838, service was taken in the lovely first school next door, itself only built 20 years earlier. Records show that boys and girls of the school were kept apart in school until 1897. It is difficult to comment on this statistic except perhaps to add that I am sure many, being of a junior age, would prefer that rule still to be in place. The Quakers, as I have mentioned before, blossomed during the 17th century and Beck Houses no doubt did well because of their local boy Francis Howgill's representation. The Beckhouses Meeting grew so quickly following Fox at Firbank that by 1708 it was able to build its own dedicated school for Quaker children. These buildings are now long closed to children and are now hidden landmarks on hidden back lanes.

LAMBRIGG WIND FARM

New visitors to the region or journeymen who have been absent for a few years will immediately notice a significant landmark on the skyline that marks the southern entrance to the Howgills. The Lambrigg Wind Farm is impossible to miss from the motorway and if you do miss it you should pull over and have a rest by taking a cup from the lonely snack bar caravan that sits in a lay-by at the motorway junction. It is almost the perfect landmark to announce a Cumbrian arrival and a bleak and windy welcome that somehow mirrors the contradiction of size and pace. I confess to liking the Lambrigg wind turbines as they tell me I am nearly home, however, they are controversial and not everyone finds them an acceptable addition.

Five huge (43 metre high) towers, each supporting massive blades (30 metres long) dominate the horizon. Hypnotising the passer-by, whether on foot or by wheel, eyes warily drift into their path and a double-whammy whirl is required in order to check their numbers, their rank and position. Simple sedentary beacons or Orwellian machines from a new dawn? A debatable question that impacts on us all.

Pitching opportunity to embrace the 21st century, the new technology and our expectant future generation the makers wisely, or cleverly at least, involved children in the launch of the windfarm in September 2000. The marketers would have held many a meeting mulling over the merits of softening the menace with the introduction of 'child'. The turbines have taken the names of local children and this extenuates their living potential. It was a drawing competition, sponsored by National Wind Power that led to the four winners from Old Hutton Primary School and one from Grayrigg Primary School who gave their names to the turbines. It is indicative of this era and one of centuries ago as we see Henry, Leanne, Charlotte, Emma and Emily spin tall.

When the wind does not stir it is easy to pretend that those great blades are only sleeping. These turbines generate electricity and it is not surprising that the imagination conjures them into mechanical monsters of Frankenstein proportions. They can generate enough power to meet the needs of around 4,000 homes a year. The £4.2 million scheme has produced the most powerful machines (1.3MW turbines) used to date at an onshore wind farm in the United Kingdom. Incredibly the blades, towers, and generators took just two weeks to install. The turbines are carefully situated at different heights on the fell to make optimum use of the landscape. This is the usual reason why you might see three moving and two still. They operate 24 hours a day and will only stop when there is poor wind, a need for routine maintenance, major work on the grid or a computer malfunction. Beneath the surface there is a more than a breeze of business and public controversy and it does not take long to dissect two distinct parties in favour and against the modern machines.

National WindPower, running their 13th site, are happy to give the media-friendly statement that 'the turbines are a step towards a more sustainable future for the UK, reducing global warming and producing a significant amount of clean energy.' The Lambrigg wind farm has not been to the liking of everyone and opposing groups such as the aforementioned FELLS (the Friends of

Eden, Lakeland and Lunesdale) have campaigned vigorously against them. A public statement exclaimed that the giant windmills are 'a horrendous blot on the landscape' and a distraction to motorists. A claim that the windfarm principles can offset around 14,000 tonnes per year of carbon dioxide emissions from what may be called traditional energy sources are countered by the antagonists with equally outstanding facts and figures. Whilst supporting the government's endeavours to produce ten per cent of the United Kingdom's energy from renewable sources by 2010, the campaigners stress that it would require 130,000 turbines of the type currently been built to meet the shortfall in power over the next decade or so.

Whether it is a gasp of amazement and delight or a sharp intake of breath in horror that greets Lambrigg, it is nothing but a gentle feather floating on the breeze compared to the storms approaching when the strong army of nearly 30 turbines of Whinash Fell come into view. Take a breath; they are not there yet. However, detailed plans are in the public domain and the dominant public is not happy. The intention to erect 27 turbines more

powerful than Lambrigg (2.0MW) would make the wind farm easily the largest land turbine development in Europe, extending over five miles in length. Lambrigg may prove to be the Trojan Horse to the outbreak of windfarmania and there can be doubt that the outbreak of turbines along the fell will change the landscape forever. The money that crosses palms in the south will always be a bigger draw to the capitalist architects than the plight of the people who actually live there. 'Not in my back yard' becomes a powerful phrase.

Pylons over Shap Fell and rows of railway terraces like at Tebay are modern architectural heirlooms. Bell-beaker mounds, rabbit pillows and the Druid circles are also scars made by man all having an impact on the landscape. Perhaps 'tattoo' is a better word than scar, as man has a habit of viewing them, at first, with mixed feelings. Certainly, at first, the 'owner' likes them and the 'observer' may be less sure. In time, opinions alter. Some tattoos remain tasteful and tell a tale of a different life, of nostalgia and of personal endeavour, of pain and of love. Other tattoos are a disaster, an irreversible mistake, an opportunity for regret, and an unwanted memory. Some people view the motorway as a horrible scar and others view it as the perfect vessel for moving people along, albeit not always with speed.

I view today's outlook with concern as man continues to make mistakes yet somehow manages to make them on a larger scale each time. How we will view the wind turbines in years to come cannot be predicted but with much of the Howgill Fells still open to infection our landscape is at risk and the purity of our freedom is open to abuse.

KILLINGTON SERVICE STATION TO PRESTON PATRICK

How marvellous to find a motorway service station that isn't heaving with my friends, the impatient and intolerant tourists. Even the sound of the motorway is softened to a gentle hum by a bank of Scots pine. Killington offers relief to only one side of the motorway and thereby, perhaps, lays its secret; a sort of calming uniformity of line. In the world of wining and dining, Killington Service Station was one of my first treats. Before chicken in a basket came in to its own and 'pub grub' took over, the family dining out was a rarity, particularly with young children. My parents brought my brother and me to Killington. In those days there was excitement at travelling on a motorway - and what a route to lose your motorway virginity - and also a thrill at eating a meal that wasn't your mothers. And

chips! We were sometimes given another option for eating out: Tebay Services on the northbound route.

Like all motorway service stations up and down the country, Killington now offers much more than mediocre meals. Today there are speciality coffee kiosks, exotic burger bars and games rooms. Strangely roomier, despite its smaller

scale, than many of its peers Killington Service Station somehow allows the driver and passenger to re-engage the brain, the limbs, and the lungs; and so, perhaps, to send them back on to the motorway in a better frame of mind for safe, uncompetitive driving.

From the seats by the windows of the inner capsule that is the café the resting driver and passenger can see Killington Reservoir. Constructed in 1817 when William Crosseley was commissioned to dig out the land on Killington Common, the purpose of the reservoir was to provide water for the Lancaster Canal. Supported by bodies such as the Countryside Commission the surrounding land is lush with native trees such as the Scots pine, oak, birch, ash and alder, along with exotic introductions such as Japanese larch, sitka and Norway spruce. Tufted ducks and Canada geese stop here on their migration, yet will step back in the pecking order allowing the huge sea gulls from the nearby coast to raid the bins and hover impatiently over gorging travellers. Indeed, these

gulls group and squawk so ferociously as they bid fearlessly for the scraps it is no wonder they are known disaffectionately as the Murder of Morecambe Crows.

Eagle eyed picnickers will look across the reservoir and notice it has two dams, one beneath the distant horizon of Middleton Fell and the other closer to the motorway. For those not wishing to treat the environment as an open prison or Grand Prix pit-stop, it is possible and permissible to wander down to the edge of the lake. The stile in the corner over the lower car park allows the motorist to detach themselves further from their journey as they can relax on the bank formed when the services were extended in 1985 and 1986.

Over the lake is a sailing club for yachts and around the islets in inlets are hides for those itching to twitch and pitching ports for those angling to fish. Indeed fishing is a thriving recreation and the Kent (Westmorland) Angling Association opens its doors to visitors as well as members.

Like many disciplined sports the rules are strict. The association stocks the lake regularly from March to October with over 5,000 rainbow trout, weighing around 1.5 lbs each. Rainbow fishing is all year round whereas brown trout is seasonal (March to September). The lake is known for its good pike fishing (with specimen fish of 20 lbs being taken) and other fish such as roach, perch and bream. Even with such numbers keenness is controlled, as there is a 'bag limit' of two fish per angler per day

The back roads from Killington village lead to a maze of winding roads, some signed some unsigned, and whilst a map is desirable it is sometimes more fun without. The motorist must expect to do some reversing and high bank riding, as opposing vehicles will compete for the narrowest of spaces. Smiles and waves are appropriate too as mutual appreciation of the difficult yet entertaining roads is realised.

Killington village is not the easiest place to find and as such we should all be grateful. A small cluster of houses and farm buildings sit amongst a tumbling brook and undulating fell. Killington Hall and All Saints Church provide tight command over the village. When safely parked, footpaths lead off at defined angles to Green Home and up to Lily Mere. The path to the hall and church leads off the road and over a slight ravine, previously home to a drawbridge. As such the buildings do not face onto the road itself but take a dramatic valley view. This makes them all the more special and immediately private, especially as the village is so secret and quiet. How different from the service station only across the fell.

From the road the hall looks derelict and the portion approached first is most definitely in serious decay. The hall used to have two substantial cross-wings; only a battered and ruined south portion stands today. It shares a style with halls at Selside and Preston Patrick and, albeit dangerous to assume, may therefore have shared the same architect and builders. This decay and the mullioned windows of the main section make it attractive to the camera.

All Saints Church was a Pickering private chapel and is notable for its splendid glass windows. Three hundred years ago another chapel stood (in Chapelgarth Close) and shared its clients with neighbouring Firbank. This site may be long gone but the sharing continues as parochial clergy

strong message to the infrequent traveller that this is a popular attraction.

The river is arguably at its most spectacular along this stretch. It is also at its most inviting and swimming in the heat of the summer sun must be tempting indeed. Strong swimmers may find it tough to take this beck in their stride. Less than confident swimmers must take heed that the water takes no prisoners. Remnant studs in a protruding rock are a memory to a diving board.

Back in the west (on the Kendal side) the roads continue to twist and turn and it is easy to lose one's bearings and perceptions of magnetic north. The signpost always seem to direct you into the thick of these narrow networks and then suddenly it disappears as if challenging instinct to decide left, right, or straight on. With a bit of luck you may find yourself at New Hutton.

priest-in-charge, Revd Anne Pitt serves Killington and Firbank (and Holy Trinity, Howgill). On a busy Sunday Revd Pitt may be seen at 9am at Killington for Holy Communion, at Firbank at ten for Morning Prayer then Howgill at eleven for more Holy Communion. It is comforting to comprehend the connection between Communion and community when a conduit chairman such as Anne links the churchgoing citizens.

You can see the sea from the road on the hill above Killington. In the other direction, the view from Aikrigg commands one of the most pastoral, panoramic and private views of the Howgill Fells. In the bottom of the valley the Lune appears again as a comfort to the compass at Killington New Bridge and a lovely walk up by the river. The gate onto the path from the road is worthy of mention if only to highlight its uniqueness. Built to accommodate pushchairs and bicycles it gives a

Devoid of bus, pub, shop or post office, the village, for a time at least had no church a decade or two ago. The Chapel of St. John is recorded to have stood in the village as long ago as 1739 yet today pride of ecclesiastical place goes to St. Stephen on the old site. Enlarged and restored in 1828 this interesting church fell into disrepair and was forced to close its doors in 1986. Dismayed by their loss, the local community were able to raise the money to give the church a second birth and it was restored and re-dedicated by the Lord Bishop of Carlisle on 14 January 1989. The church interior is brightly lit with natural light because of its aspect on the fell and the stained glass windows are refreshingly vivid beside the plain white walls. A ceramic cross offers more colour and reflective manner as it hangs from the eastern wall as a gift from the local schoolchildren to celebrate Queen Elizabeth's Golden Jubilee in 2002. Then outside, the visitor once more bows with eyes warily blinking upwards to the high ornamental dogs that guard the gate pillars. Our Hutton enquiry need not stop here, as Old Hutton is worthy of trial too.

Heading back along the lanes, one route comes out at Preston Patrick and another famous Quaker Meeting House. The Friends at Preston Patrick were influential in the early days and played an important part in the foundation Quaker ethics.

Following George Fox's arrival and a wide acceptance of his ideals, many of the convinced sought to find easier, softer ways and others attempted to make matters more complex. The Preston Patrick Friends retreated somewhat and held their meetings in secret. The reason being that two of their sons, John Wilkinson of Millholme and John Story of Goosegreene, were disruptive across Britain prompting anti-Fox feeling and causing a division that became known as the Wilkinson-Story schism of 1673, derived from an interesting publication called *The Spirit of the Hat*. By 1680 all serious divisions were healed and the Preston Patrick Friends were able to focus on building a dedicated Meeting House. This

something more about the Lancaster Canal and I will. Strangely, an increase in ship size was the prompt for the building of the canal. The newer larger ships of the mid-18th century could not navigate the notorious Lune estuary and trade was being lost to Liverpool from prosperous Lancaster. The local traders contracted John Rennie (1761-1821) to survey the route and although dogged by financial problems the canal was eventually through to Kendal in 1826, some 34 years after work started and four years after Rennie's death. Rennie, incidentally, designed and supervised the building of Waterloo Bridge, London (1810-17), Southwark Bridge (1814-19) and the new London Bridge.

The trip from Kendal to Preston by packet boat took eight hours. Even a bad day on the present-day motorway is unlikely to be this long. The

they did, in 1691, to a style that was clearly very similar in design to nearby Briggflatts (1674). It was significantly repaired and restored in 1869 with additional buildings of schoolroom, coach house and stable added to complement the size of the local fellowship.

Above Preston Patrick, and always seen from the motorway is the church with the neon beacon. At dusk when the light has faded so that the land is all but gone, a single cross lights up this small hill as if to call people to God's own country. For me it is a striking reminder that I am almost home.

Around Preston Patrick and Crooklands the landscape opens up once more and the next motorway junction provides a reminder that the real world still exists. Crooklands is itself just a bend in the Kendal road now although the very fine Lancaster Canal offers some great photography, as canals do. It is too tempting an opportunity to say

growth of the Lancaster and Carlisle Railway forced the demise of the canal and in 1944 the upper section to Kendal was closed and later, as the M6 was built in the 1960s, much of it was drained leaving only 42 of the original 57 miles of canal intact and running from Tewitfield to Preston. The canal today remains unique as it is a contour canal and as such has no locks. It has only been linked with other waterways in the last twelve months, after a wait of approaching 200 years, thanks to the opening of the Millennium Ribble Link; a new four-mile link includes seven new canal locks, one river lock and one sea lock. Predictably, there are plans to re-invent it further with a £50 million scheme running to restore the Kendal connection.

The canal's relevance to the Howgills is one of supply. Lying 750 feet above sea level Killington Reservoir supplies up to 3.7 million gallons of water per day to the canal at the Crooklands feeder point. It is one of the largest canal feeders in the country. Being over the motorway in the west and only six miles from Kendal this is dangerously close to being outside of my brief, yet worthy of a snapshot visit whatever your goal.

Prepare yourself for an imaginary prayer circuit and take a tour around the lost and lovely small churches and chapels of the network between Sedbergh and Kirkby Lonsdale. Indeed do not imagine it, do it. I have found that by doing church tours such as this, I pick up the spiritual meaning of faith, strength and hope by realising the effort people, of yesterday and today, have gone through to seek and support their chosen God.

The monks of the Praemonstratensian Order did their own tour from Preston Patrick. After setting up an abbey at Preston Patrick in 1119, it was deemed not as good a place for religion as the fields below Shap and so their monastery was moved in 1199 to what we now know as Shap Abbey. Many sources give differing dates for the origins at Preston Patrick and move to Shap, some saying 1191 and 1201, some 1122 and 1125. I would surmise that all have an element of truth, with decisions being agreed, deferred, agreed and so on; much in same way as the planning committees of the councils of today.

I have to thank Bert Whalley (*Cumbria,* February 1998, Vol 47 No 11) for researching the headstones at St. Patrick's at Preston Patrick and confirming the notoriety of some of the folk laid to rest there. How else would we know of Sir Herbert Barker, born at Lupton Tower who pioneered orthopedic shoes; or Jim Hutchinson who as a clothier made lifelong breeches and sold them for the princely sum of £15; and Colonel Oliver North, presumably an ancestor of the current day American anti-hero.

The paths, lanes and roads from Preston Patrick to Kirkby Lonsdale repeat similar names of homes we have already come across further north. These places are no less significant: Hollins, Borrens, Kiln Hall, Carlingwha, Badgergate, Cow Brow, Hellgill, and a little to the south another Docker. We also have High Row, Middle Row, Low Row and High Fell, Middle Fell and Low Fell. In some ways this similarity makes the area more distinct and one can see an ancient natural community boundary limited by the smallest of today's distances.

KIRKBY LONSDALE

Kirkby Londsdale folk refer to their hometown as Kirkby. So do folk from Kirkby Stephen and those from Kirkby Thore and so too those from other towns nomenclaturely inclined towards their church. On the whole confusion is avoided between the 'Kirkbys' by adequate distance and scale.

The name Kirkby, formed from the Norse *kirkja*, church, and *byr*, settlement, is usually understood to have been given to towns where the church was already in existence when the Norse arrived. Kirkbys do have a tendency to be important and may have grown to be market towns of significance even if their names change over the years, for example, Kendal used to Kirkby Kendal and St. Bees, Kirkby Beecock. On the other side of the Howgill Fells, in the south as Kirkby Stephen is to the north, sits Kirkby Lonsdale.

The Church of St. Mary the Virgin is at the heart of Kirkby Lonsdale and offers a great feast of odd

corners to attract the visitor. Dating from the 11th century the church and its immediate surroundings have gathered in many architectural crops that the meal is too big for one solitary serving. I can only give a taste here. Inside St. Mary's diamond dating has helped to age the pleasing Norman pillars to the early 12th century. The diamond patterns that give the pillars their uniqueness are recognisable as sisters to those in Durham Cathedral where dating is confirmed between 1096 and 1115.

Two hundred years ago a parishioner of some pull insisted on a pillar being removed because it restricted his pulpit view. This prize pillar of the community so commonly displaying ungodly egoism had his wish and the pillar was removed and reset in a corner of a house elsewhere in town by Fairbank. A replacement pillar was installed some 60 years later; presumably after the demise of the complainant. Further enquiry at a western pillar reveals a carving of a foliated 'Green Man'. I have been interested in Green Men for some time and their ecclesiastical existence in such Christian households holds a contradiction with their pagan polytheistic origins.

Of further interest inside is the baptismal font,

which originates from Killington. Beginning life in the 14th century chapel at Killington, the font found its way into a field as a water trough when the chapel needed it no more. Some 70 or 80 years ago it was discovered and presented to St Mary's, duly reconsecrated and used for baptisms once more. Provider of water for life throughout its career.

And so to the outside of St Mary's and the striking sight of the tower that greets the wide-eyed visitor. The symmetry of the wings to either side is skewed by the positioning of the clock-face. Whatever church clock do we know with a face so superficially lazily lowered on a tower? Looking like an afterthought at first the faces on two walls of the tower sit to one side like jigsaw pieces waiting to be securely fixed. There was a rumour that the faces were slipped to the lower side of the two towers to make them visible to their benefactor

whose rooms could only see them if in this position. An unlikely tale at first glance is made more believable when we come to consider how seriously Kirkby natives take their views. The clock faces date from 1810 and are more likely to be in their current position because of the clock mechanism inside the tower. This mechanism was donated in 1911 by J R Pickard, churchwarden from 1906 to 1923, as a tribute to King Edward VII.

It may be unkind to offer a derogatory opinion of any part of Kirkby Lonsdale, yet I am not over enamoured by Ruskin's View at the edge of the church gardens above the river. Yes, it is special. Yes, it is outstanding. However, I do question its uniqueness. Move along a hundred yards and the view is better. This may only be because if you do move along you will find yourself standing on your own and not next to the touring mob who have no courage to stand to one side for fear of solitary independence. Ruskin, who was not one to ignore controversy or to agree for want of appearing to conform, stole the tourist name from the artist Turner who had taken his own liking to the vista and refined it onto canvas (Kirkby Lonsdale Churchyard 1818) just as today's visitors hurriedly commit it to film, whatever the weather. To think that today's Kodak traveller's get home and show their friends skewed pictures proclaiming it to be what Ruskin saw sends a shudder down my spine. You

know me well enough already to understand that I only care because it keeps the world going around.

Ruskin, of course, was a great publicist and must have convinced the tourist office of the day that Ruskin's View had more marketability than Turner's View. A quick thinking TIC manager would have labelled it Turner's View and labelled something else with Ruskin's name. Ruskin's Corner perhaps? Or maybe Turner's Corner and Ruskin's View? I don't know, maybe I have given you ideas of your own. That ramble aside, why didn't Ruskin simply turnaround? The churchyard is one of the most splendid and restful, especially in the spring when the daffodils and crocuses dominate so. The 18th century gazebo may be but a folly yet it is an architectural delight. As too is the superb rectory, built in 1783 and expanded upwards in the 1830s.

My antithesis towards tourism is flawed and I cannot help but take a diversion down the route of history to help explain the relationship between wordsmiths, artists and tourists. At Kirkby Lonsdale we have seen a slight between Turner and Ruskin. The significance towards the very invention of tourism is to be seen at the same time and in the hands of William Wordsworth. Wordsworth is often credited with single-handedly starting the

Wordsworth, meanwhile, was not fond of tourists it seems and having been away, returned to live at Dove Cottage in 1799 where he was 'disgusted by the degree to which the impact of visitors had changed the landscape... particularly dismayed by the construction for off-comers of unsuitably designed and located villas.'

Even today, the Turner's View courts controversy continues. Towards the end of 2003 local farmer Thomas Wharton was refused planning permission to convert a barn, lying on the horizon of Turner's View, into three residential properties. South Lakeland District Council ruled that his proposed development detracted from the landscape. Mr Wharton in comic revenge painted his barn in

tourist explosion in the Lake District with his many works including his *Guide to the Lakes*; but did this trigger a desire for the 'sightseer'? It appears not. Ian Whyte in his excellent paper titled *Picturesque Tourism* (2000) notes that in the late 18th century 'picturesque' meant a view that would not only look good in a picture but one that was painted by a specific group of painters based out of Rome, notably Rosa, Poussin and Lorrain. The picturesque tourist began to compare his views with the art form from Italy and, quite rightly, tourism appreciation was born through comparison of what had been witnessed before. We learn then that, apart from again having to thank the Italians for something, the appreciation of Turner's View depends on what else you have seen.

bright stripes of colours. The reds, blues, and yellows turned the barn into a giant Liquorice Allsort and made the national headlines. As one critic was heard to retort "Turner Prizes have been given for less!"

The rest of Kirkby offers plenty of treats for the traveller and many more ancient sites and views. It is a very picturesque place and postcard collectors among you will recognise a weightier fistful of second hand cards hidden away at collectors' fairs originating from Kirkby Lonsdale than from nearby Sedbergh and Kirkby Stephen. The Market Square offers itself to be photographed as circular cloisters entertain the fidgety bottoms of potentially troublesome youths looking for amusement. The picture cannot be taken without stray cars and white vans; signposts, litter bins and traffic cones; adolescent school kids stealing a smoke and the elderly pausing for breath - perhaps today's aesthetic displeases but it will capture a different eye tomorrow. Just as our eyes captured those scenes of a century ago, today's picture will seem ancient and dated in years to come.

I must try to photograph the street furniture and bystanders of the day as they happen in full normal view as well as being patiently intent on capturing stone scenes free of people and ornament. I must also try and be more sympathetic to the plight of our youth (I was one after all, and still attempt to cast a young shadow) and I cannot help but praise the youngsters of the Queen Elizabeth School in Kirkby for capturing Ruskin's View as the title for their newsletter cum journal appended to the community news. Inspired and clearly talented. I also raise my hat to the curious conglomeration, on 10

August 2003, of an outdoor Parisian style exhibition launched by the Churchmouse Cheeses company under the resurrecting title of The First Annual Kirkby Lonsdale Turner Day.

Kirkby Lonsdale is not of course, the property of the tourist. It is home for many and the locals do embrace the town. Indeed, even with windy roads in all directions, Kirkby Lonsdale is popular for many living out of the immediate town. Kirkby Lonsdale could be called 'trendy'. Whether wanting speciality cheeses or cuddly teddy bears people regularly travel from Settle to the east and from Carnforth in the west. In between their keen shopping and coffee shop stopping, they can step out and visit an odd corner on each visit.

Eighty six steep steps down to the river from the churchyard corner near Ruskin's View give the visitor a 'radically' different view and takes an inquisitive rambler past Lardy and Fishery Brow to Devil's Punch Bowl. The Devil seems to be keen to be seen in Kirkby Lonsdale. Along the riverbank and the Devil's Bridge is soon in eyeline between the over-hanging trees. It would be remiss of me to criticise Devil's Bridge with such cynicism as I did Ruskin's View, yet I do beg a question - what is all the fuss about? Devil's Bridge is no doubt a marvellous and picturesque structure with an excellent legend to justify its place as the major landmark of Kirkby Lonsdale. The Lune has many bridges and many are mentioned in this book. No other bridge obtains the attention like this one. I am sure just as many people look at, and even photograph as a backdrop, neighbouring Stanley Bridge but I am sure the majority do not know it is the name of the road bridge that stands below the tourist attraction.

For the record, St. Mary's shares the Romanesque architecture of the bridge and the same Norman masons are clearly responsible for both structures. Local expert David Smail supposes that it probably took about 60 skilled masons to build the bridge, originally known as Kirkby Bridge until the 19th century. Mr Smail also confirms that the modern name for the bridge is not unique to ours in Kirkby Lonsdale and river crossings around the globe share the same mysterious tale.

The legend of Devil's Bridge is worthy and enjoys minor changes depending on whom you listen to or what you read. One story goes that a woman waiting for her husband to return home discovered the river awash and too deep to cross. The Devil appeared offering a bridge in exchange for a soul, the first to take a step on his structure. The husband duly came into sight and being accompanied by his dog had good fortune to see his dog run to greet his wife and thus become the foiled prey for the Devil, who ashamed and defeated departed leaving his new bridge.

Others are varieties on a theme, many without the husband, and some giving the woman good sense to throw bait for the dog thus urging him into the Devil's trap. Others mention the woman losing her only cow to the other side of the river when she was too afraid to wade after it. You can choose your favourite to pass on to your grandchildren. Such tales fire the imagination, especially when concerning our icon of fear.

The bridge's undeniable standing and age do warrant the many visitors it receives and if it acts as a catalyst to bringing people to the town and district then I hold my hands up to its validity in today's necessary tourist climate. Perhaps it is named Devil's Bridge because it is a magnet to tourists and their need to be with tobacco, toilets, tea, toast and trouble.

I find little peace here and sometimes the only picturesque thing I see is the row of gleaming motorbikes and their riders. Coming here since the first bikes were used to get out and about, Devil's Bridge has become one of the most popular meeting places for the new horses and their

warning badge beyond Stanley Bridge is a homemade pier of some stature. Stanley's boundaries are invisible as he goes unnoticed doing his traffic-supporting business. Whether Stanley Bridge entertains the public as long as Devil's Bridge has done is uncertain and it does depend if Stanley's colleagues in council were corrupt with their cement. Some would say that our 20th century architects have spurious claims to longevity; I guess we will cross that bridge when we come to it.

riders. Sunday morning and riders from all over the country set off a day's tour. The first part of the ride is to Devil's Bridge to gather the spirit and soul of the saddled companion. The next journey sees an explosion of routes over high fell and down dale as literally thousands of miles are covered.

One team goes up and through Pennine Alston, another over Lakeland Kirkstone, another Stainmore and Scotch Corner, another skirt around Skipton, another to surf at Grange, and more. At the end of the day they may return to the bridge to give a nod to a fine day and to share tales of the road. I wonder if many people now come to watch the motormen and motorwomen and their machines rather than to enter into the mind of the lady, her dog and Old Nick?

The sign reads 'No Bathing, No Canoeing, No Fishing,' yet 100 yards from the tree holding this

LUNE HALLS, HOMES AND HOUSES

My drift about Kirkby Lonsdale has been to attempt to explain that I hope visitors see more than Ruskin's View and Devil's Bridge. I am sure they will. There are other architectural delights and scenic settings to satisfy the Lune guest. Not far from the view along by the river is Underley Hall, one of many noble halls and mansions in the valley; elevated examples of the wealth and well being of the landlords and landowners that have always tenured their roots in the land.

Halls and manors dominate the landscape here; Barbon Manor, Rigmaden, Mansergh, Kirfit and further down to Hornby Castle and finally to Cockersands Abbey. Many are farms and presumably always have been and truly earn a deserved living. Indeed, to take two examples we find ourselves walking humbly beside current occupants. Today, Underley Hall continues in the broader aspect of education developed across the whole of this region with astounding expertise, by focusing on 24 hour special needs of vulnerable boys and girls who need particular help with confidence, relationships and reasons of anxiety. Their fine words not mine.

Underley Hall was erected by Alexander Nowell, in 1825 and cost the not insignificant sum of about £30,000. The house is made of yellow freestone and has had a number of modifications during its lifetime, notably in 1872 with the addition of a 100 foot tower and a conservatory of 70 feet by 20. This rehabilitation took three years and cost £10,000. A private bridge links Underley to the east bank of the Lune and was built for essential communication with Barbon Railway Station.

The bridge is built to a Roman Gothic style, features two ribbed arches with a span of around 70 feet making them the largest ribbed arches in the

country. The link to the railway is slight now and even the Underley Hall steam train, number 6928, built in 1941, withdrawn from service in 1965, has been long since been scrapped. The train may or may not have pulled cattle trucks in its time. Had it passed Underley, it may have collected some of the celebrated shorthorn cattle known as the Underley Darlings.

Maintaining livestock links, Mansergh Hall is a farm dedicated to the production of lamb and like Underley is clearly gifted at its chosen discipline. Four generations of Hadwin families have cared for the estate and the fifth generation of Hadley children are also keenly involved. The farm grassland is sole host to the lamb so that they can adequately control the use of semi-organic fertiliser and prevent the use of any herbicides or pesticides. The owners are keen to publicise the flock as being kept under scrutiny for 'total consideration' towards the animal's welfare. The advertising blurb stretches to mighty claims of leanest and tenderest and tastiest.

The FoodUK (Lamb) Guide, for what it's worth, lists Mansergh Hall Lamb among the top seventeen producers and comes highly recommended by top chef, William Drabble. Drabble, who replaced Gordon Ramsey as head chef of the London restaurant Aubergine, quoted in a Sunday newspaper, "I buy my lamb from Mansergh Hall Farm... The meat is absolutely exquisite, full of flavour and incredibly tender." Farming, whether it is animal husbandry or 'modern energy techniques' as in the eerily and appropriately named Lambrigg Wind Farm, is notoriously controversial, as activists seek to air their views swept away by emotion and hungry for change.

I enjoy listening to the debates of both sides whether vegans or omnivores, atheists or pluralists, cavemen or spacemen, and healthy controversy will, with common ground, lead us to proper outcomes.

Controversy is a form of co-operative thinking. The only object of engaging in it is to persuade our audience or our readers of what we believe to be the truth. For this purpose it is necessary to assume that we have some common ground with them, and even (if possible) with our opponents, as the basis on which argument can proceed. Otherwise controversy is a waste of time. This may seem a truism. It would be so if there were not a type of controversialist frequently met with whose concern seems to be chiefly to display his wit, his learning, or his ingenuity. Now these are qualities of which the possessor may justly be proud, but unless allied to common sense and balance they are apt to prove a snare. Such display may amuse, dazzle, and even nonplus the listener; but it makes no converts worth winning, and is a liability rather than an asset to a movement it seeks to serve... Where men are fighting for their lives, or for some cause dearer to them than life, weapons are out and no quarter is given; but among friendly disputants such displays are out of place. Away from the life-and-death struggle, away from the political arena, the controversialist should practice the virtues appropriate to co-operative thinking. He should acknowledge his own limitations and, in the words of Oliver Cromwell 'think it possible that he may be mistaken'.

Archibald Robertson, *Art of Controversy*, Rationalist Annual, 1943

Many, if not all, of these special farmhouses and manor buildings gave themselves labels to satisfy their egos and prove their worth. Extravagant and stylish additions made each home unique, at the very least to the eye of the stonemason. The same mason would be subtler in adding his own stamp of craftsmanship with initials or symbols in hidden corners. Each artefact, large or small, is now a prize for the keen spy.

J H Palmer's wonderful book *Historic Farmhouses in and around Westmorland* (1946) takes us to some 50 such homes, too many to mention here. However, a few caught my eye such as the mason's mark of a swastika at Fowlstone Farm, Lupton, near Kirkby Lonsdale and a horse in low relief on a stone tablet in the stable wall of Greenlane Farm, also Lupton.

Other halls have different curiosities. Kirfit Hall at Casterton boasts a ghostly tale of a headless woman who wanders the grounds, doing nobody any harm, as her original purpose was to scare Henry VIII when he was 'courting' local girl, Katherine Parr. Middleton Hall holds vital proof for my theory about the pessimism of us northern types. Painted above a door in the 'withdrawing-room' are the Latin words *ventrum exhoresco diem* or 'I dread the coming day'. We seem to delight in pessimism and as such we are rarely disappointed.

Whether Victorian or Edwardian or, as now, 21st century high flyers, the noble and rich have an eye for the beauty and suitability of fine

countryside for setting up a grand home. Today's nobility may not have exactly the same wealth as yesteryear and their feast may be from a shorter term of business success, but their ability to escape the maddening crowd is not diminished. Today we find the commuter sets up home in new detached houses or farmhouse conversions before travelling to work in Manchester, Newcastle and Glasgow. I believe this to be absolutely fine as long as they contribute to the local economy and use the local amenities and, in time, become local too.

LECK BECK, COWAN BRIDGE

I have to admit to unfamiliarity to the area surrounding Kirkby Lonsdale and by that I mean the tracks and paths are familiar but I have no intimacy with tips and tricks of trekking over them. I do not know which farmers are grumpy, which farmers are friendly, which fences are barbed, and which earth is wet. The pathways in the whole region are, generally welcoming, yet experience can make a difference even when a simple outing is on the agenda. Taking the lead from Mr R A C Lowndes in his reading on *Celtic Fields in the Lune Valley* (CWAAS 1962) I have recently taken a tour, delayed by some 41 years, of the ancient sites between Kirkby and Sedbergh. The tour makes an excellent itinerary today, as I am sure it did then.

The road from Kirkby Lonsdale to Sedbergh via Casterton is faster than it should be and many drivers, like those at Orton, seem to turn into Grand Prix racers as they swing swiftly into corner and out again. Those wanting a more leisurely look at this shallow valley with tempting fells may do worse than to take the narrow road that runs parallel to the busier trunk route. Of course, if able, on foot is better still.

The narrow road more closely approximates the route taken by the Romans and a good map will have you scratching your head as to why their straight and direct method was ignored in favour of the 20th century chicanes. Going out and over Stanley Bridge there may be an instinct to turn back towards the Howgills and the signposted immediacy of Casterton. First, though, to allow a complete education to unfold, it is worth a three-mile detour to Cowan Bridge on the Ingleton road.

Cowan Bridge lies nearby Casterton yet because of these new routes pegged by turnpikes, and dissected by railways and elsewhere by canals and motorways, ancient familiarity is challenged as dimensional geometry is upended. Just as Grayrigg no longer is as close a neighbour to Firbank, now Cowan Bridge sits at a busy road junction away from Casterton.

Its relationship with Casterton must be now diminished although it will often be reminded of its links because of the very special old girls of its school. A small plaque on the (private) house wall near the three bridges of Cowan Bridge, two of which are now beyond their original intention, gives notification of the Bronte connection. If your literary expertise takes you in this direction then you will recognise Cowan Bridge as the host to Lowood from *Jane Eyre* by Charlotte Bronte.

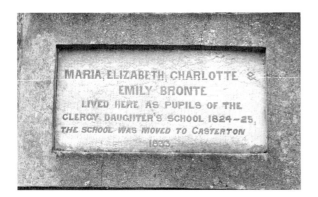

The Bronte sisters attended the Clergy Daughters' School a year after it opened between 1824 and 1825. It is said that Charlotte was only eight when she attended the school and her memories of the place were dramatically coloured by the departure from the school of her sisters Maria and Elizabeth because of terminal illness. Her bitter vision was based on resentment and we can assume that the Clergy Daughters' School was not as savage as she portrayed. I hardly think any of the sisters would recognise the place today.

Sadly the plaque is dusty and grey, as is the rest of the wall as it faces the road to be showered with road silt and exhaust smoke as rubber wheels burn by without noticing. Lowood was depicted as having a harsh regime yet I fear the vision is now compromised by another harsh regime of impatient traffic. Although surrounded by fell, the air is of lowland and the drama befits a different texture, a different civility, than that of the upland in my perimeter to the Howgill Fells.

It is often written that Charlotte Bronte may

have borne resentment at a miserable time at Cowan Bridge and translated this emotion into her vision of Lowood. I would warrant a subtlety different interpretation, as I think she used her own hardship there to draw on an inherent optimism to improve and turn the experience into the inspiration and career that made her name. Learning by the folly of others and embracing her mentors, she recognised and accepted the need for altered attitudes, for change, for progress. This is implicit in her writing of the time:

The school, thus improved, became in time a truly useful and noble institution. I remained an inmate of its walls, after regeneration, for eight years - six as a pupil, and two as a teacher; and in both capacities I bear my testimony to its value and importance. During these eight years my life was uniform, but not unhappy, because it was not inactive. I had means of an excellent education placed within my reach; a fondness for some of my studies, and a desire to excel in all, together with a great delight in pleasing my teachers, especially such as I loved, urged me on. I availed myself fully of the advantages offered me. In time I rose to be the first girl of the first class; then I was invested with the office of teacher; which I discharged with zeal for two years; but at the end of that time I altered.

The shop, store and post office in Cowan Bridge hide the turning to Leck. R A C Lowndes uses Leck

to illustrate the temperate strength of the valley by handing us a palm tree in a Leck garden. It is a very beautiful hamlet and different from many of the others as it appears, at least to me, to have no centre. Yet it does have a heart, as an interesting walled enclosure, almost heart-shaped, is the focus of converging Leck lanes. Lowndes continues his Leck trek to Leck Beck and up to the castle remains on Castle Hill.

His examination was more qualified than mine yet I do appreciate why his exploration was made so fascinating. The round earthwork mound sits atop a 'flat-topped spur' and is no doubt a good spot for a castle. Facing south with fells on nearly three sides it commands a sound defence, but against whom? I will let the reader work out who would seek refuge and who would be fighting to

THE ANIMALS ACT 1971
PROTECTION OF LIVESTOCK AGAINST DOGS

YOUR DOG COULD BE SHOT IF FOUND AMONGST SHEEP

knowledge I expected to be guided along simple and pleasant paths. Not so, there seems to be a deterrent of difficulty determined to deter the curious from going further. Even taking the lower path next to Leck Beck, gate signs exclaiming, 'your dog could be shot' make the adventurer somewhat wary.

Further up the hillside and on to Leck and Casterton Fells the landscape becomes potholed with challenges for the underground tourist. From Big Meanie on one side to Bullpot on the other a different breed takes to these fells and it becomes very much part of the Yorkshire Dales. As the names imply, darker and meaner.

get in. While considering keeper and invader, it is noticed that the moat is inside the castle walls. Actually, it is not as dramatic as I describe for it is a shallow mound surrounding a slight dip (Lowndes calls it a bank outside a ditch).

Indeed the whole area of the castle would hardly be big enough to secure villagers and their animals for any length of time against antagonists with any endeavour. It is at this point that the archaeologist seeks to compare his find with discoveries elsewhere in the nation. There are similar earth patterns in old Westmorland at Dufton, Kirkby Stephen (Croglin) and Waitby but these tend to exhibit huts within the circles thus confirming habitation. The theory is that Castle Hill at Leck is closer in design to the many ring-forts in Ireland, which were used as stock holdings to 'enclose domestic animals and exclude wild ones'. Of course it could be an expensive folly erected by nobles of the vale.

The land is in a conservation area and with that

CASTERTON

Keeping to the fell side and off Fell Road, which links High Casterton with Bullpott on Hoggs Hill lays another remnant of the past, the Druid Circle. Even with 20 stones around a foot high the best views are not, from within the circle, but from a higher vantage, where the natural aura of the ancient stones can be appreciated more fully. If the light is right and the eyes are working squint-free, fine valley views with Casterton and Kirkby Lonsdale in the foreground confirm the end of fell line and the squirming meander of the Lune as it lays fertile soil before stirring subtle sands at Morecambe. Some evidence exists to suggest that there has been a Bell Beaker people burial site at the circle of stones.

Until I started looking at these stone circles, and you will call me a mug for this, I had not heard of the Bell Beaker folk. Coming from the Chalcolithic Period (3000-1500 BC) they were so named because of their distinctive bell shaped drinking vessels. They were also incredibly well travelled and they supposedly arrived in Britain via Cornwall collecting on their way plenty of copper and tin. Clearly a friendly crowd, the Bell Beaker families mixed well with our Neolithic farmers and pottery bell beakers are found in many well known megalithic tombs, temples and barrows such as Stonehenge and Avebury. They are more associated with Wessex culture than Westmorland Countrymen.

Bell Beaker people preferred open sites for graves, often under a mound of stones, and are noted for extravagant grave goods like memorial battle-axes and sharp metal daggers, elaborately decorated with precious amber and gold. Some of the gold found in ancient graves is thought to be so like those of Mycenae that it suggests some foreign trade between Britain and Greece.

Fellfoot Road is host to more work by Andy Goldsworthy and these unfold as quite different from his other pieces of 'flock art'. Here they are not sheepfolds or cone pinfolds by name, but drove folds as they sit in alternation along the contoured lane that forms the lowest line along the west side of Brownthwaite. Each of the sixteen sheepfolds along the Fellfoot Drove Road contains a large boulder.

Recently I met a couple walking who were

clearly not from these parts, by a few hundred miles, who excitedly wanted to point me in the direction of the Fellfoot boulders. Stuttering with excitement they unveiled their theory that the structures cannot be natural and must be man-made!

This may or may not be the response that Goldsworthy is expecting. I do hope that these walkers also noticed the 'living' hurdles along the short route. To me, the still-in-use steel gated sheepfolds and the crumbling walls around small tired copses are as profound.

Casterton in the valley below is, like the other villages in this stretch, a hotch-potch of dispersed properties and with such dispersion it is hard to calculate a castle giving its name to the town, yet that is what Casterton quite obviously means. The church, Holy Trinity, commands the corner of the main road and is worth a visit. I found it particularly difficult to photograph as, unlike its neighbours at Middleton and Barbon, it sits surrounded by the dispersed housing! I found the best place to stand was the middle of the road and that cannot be recommended.

The church was built by that marvellously named, Reverend William Wilson Carus-Wilson, who ten years earlier had founded the Clergy Daughters' School at Cowan Bridge. In the same year, 1833, the school moved into a purpose-built establishment in Casterton. Casterton's claim to fame is largely the school, and even though its origins are at Cowan Bridge, it has been at Casterton where the school has thrived or at least been recognised by the history books. Unlike Sedbergh, which we see later relies on fame governed by wealth; Casterton's beginnings have

been humble by initially taking daughters from clergymen with the smallest incomes, educating servants, and even young orphans. The school was reconstituted in 1921 and opened its doors wider than clerical sources. Casterton School today, which I am sure has comparable values of a sound ethical education, still boards girls but also, presumably through financial necessity, welcomes boys.

In 2003, Casterton School achieved some regional notoriety by quarantining its pupils on their return from home leave. Many, it transpired, had their homes in the Far East and were potential carriers of the deadly SARS virus (Severe Acute Respiratory Syndrome thought to be caused by a mutant coronavirus) which at the time was taking on epidemic proportions across the other side of the world and becoming a worrying global risk. However small and safe we want to be there will be no escape from Armageddon.

Holy Trinity cost £750 to build. Another £600 was spent on improvements in 1865 and then restoration is reported as soon as 1891. This latter change may have been due to local demand as only three years earlier, in 1888, Casterton was given its own parish, free from Kirkby Lonsdale. Even now over a century on, I can still see those 'Dibley-like' debates as parochial councils clamber to conceive chaplain, choir and Casterton church continuity. Their independent success continued until the turbulent over-excited governments of the 1970s contrived to mix boundaries, buildings and belongings giving Holy Trinity back to Kirkby Lonsdale securities. I am sure to be sounding ecumenical with the truth with my rapid analysis of parochial past and I am not really qualified to express opinion, as I am sure the team ministry at Kirkby Lonsdale is superb at managing resources and praise at the seven colourful churches in the group.

The churchyard at Holy Trinity provides a special space to get off the road and ponder the lives that have been led before we hurried from here to there and back. The caring Carus-Wilson family are commemorated in a vault in the top of the graveyard and a curious eye will also discover a number of pupil's graves from the mid-19th century.

If the name of William Wilson Carus-Wilson brought a titter from the back of the classroom then so would Henry Holiday of Hampstead. Henry Holiday was a stained glass artist of some fame and was responsible for the splendid east and west windows and the interesting and unusual wall paintings inside the church. Born on 17 June 1839 in London, Henry Holiday made frequent trips to Cumbria and it served to introduce him to the influential figures of our old friend John Ruskin (often staying at his home at Brantwood) and Sir Edward Burnes-Jones. He also took good company with artisans Dante Gabriel Rossetti and Simeon Solomon. He went on to design his own Hawkshead home, called Betty Fold, in 1908, and applying his artistic talents to other works such as *Dante and Beatrice* and the illustrations in Lewis Carroll's *The Hunting of the Snark*. As an aside, yet complimentary in the silly names brogue, Oscar Gnosspelius, on whom the *Swallows and*

Amazons character "Squashy Hat" is based, once owned Betty Fold. You can stop giggling at the back of the classroom now.

Henry Holiday deserves to be better known. Eschewing the sentimentality and archaism of his peers, his stained glass designs are strong and dramatic, and reveal a brilliant understanding of the use of colour. Alistair MacDonald, *The Stained Glass of Henry Holiday*, 1998

Casterton's links to education are rooted in its genealogy and its current schooling principles prove that the bough is hard to break. I am indebted to Malcolm Fielding of Lonsdale College, University of Lancaster, for giving me a nice link to the next piece on Barbon and more diverse education from his 1995 dissertation on *A Social History of Natural Philosophers and Scientists in North-West England, 1780-1880*. In 1766 Thomas Garnett was born at Casterton. At the age eleven he was using a self-made dial and quadrant to measure the height of Barbon Fell.

Before summarising the rest of his career it is worth introducing John Dawson of Garsdale (1734-1820). Self educated, he used money made from the well-known local knitting houses to purchase books, and he concentrated on mathematics. By his mid 20s he was tutoring Cambridge entrants and later was to obtain his own medical qualification at Edinburgh and London. Dawson's mathematical talent identified errors in Newton's method, and 'he correctly predicted that only by observing the orbit of Venus could an accurate measure of solar distance be made'.

What better place to observe the stars than lying on the top of any one of these fells and dale tops on a warm cloud-free summer evening? He used his talents to teach and exemplary students were Thomas Garnett (apprenticed to him in 1781), Adam Sedgwick (father of geology from Dent) and Haygarth. There is a bust of Dawson inside St. Andrew's Church in Sedbergh.

Garnett was educated at Barbon till he was fifteen, when he went to Dawson as an apprentice. He then studied at Edinburgh before becoming Professor of Chemistry, Natural Philosophy and Mathematics in the new Royal Institution, in 1799. Fielding's work tells us that Garnett even transposed that huge hurdle of us northern souls and 'despite his regional accent being somewhat inharmonious to an audience in London, he made a great impact there.' What inspires me from the relationship between Dawson and Garnett is that it is clearly a great example of the power of the enthusiast to inspire and simply reading about them gives me heart to develop and facilitate and share and collaborate and progress, even now as I sit in the foothills of middle age.

BARBON AND MIDDLETON

A keen map-reader will notice an escape route away from the Lune when we reach Barbon. From Barbon village heading east to the South Lord's Land and eventually to delightful Dent, Barbondale offers many places to pull off the road and take refuge in babbling brook and sweet sedge. The area around Blindbeck Bridge is a child's dreamland of stepping-stones and water-falls, dams and fords, and perilous leaps and dar-ing rescues. Tempting even for adults skipping and hopping to the other side of Barbon Beck only pausing to take an anxious calculation of risk for the return journey, which strangely seems more difficult.

My only comment, and it is not a complaint, is that this valley always seems to be busy. That said, there is always room and with like minds seeking peace on the roadside pasture, courtesy befriends the adventure. Passing sheep may even display curiosity as deckchairs, God forbid, are removed from car boots, rugs and blankets are laid down, and the best memories of picnics from

days long gone are rekindled with timeless pleasure.

As Barbondale disappears into the Yorkshire Dales and the stunning scenery of Dentdale so do that mysterious breed of potholers. Anxious to be on their backs in dark cramped damp places these lovers of confined spaces have found their heaven above Barbondale. Bull Pot of the Witches descending to some 85 feet and Cow Pot only five feet less are the gateways to a different adventure. We will meet these dim descendants again when we cross the River Rawthey above Sedbergh in later pages.

It almost goes without saying that Barbondale is host to another Goldsworthyfold. Jack's Fold is set between the road and the beck where, on the other side of the fell, woodland opens to a walled field called Postern Hill. Jack's Fold was first built for the 1996 launch of the Sheepfolds

Project at the University of Hertfordshire in the deepest south climes of St. Albans before being freed back into its natural northern habitat.

Barbon is another parish in the Lonsdale belt of churches and a very pleasant hamlet befitting its rounded name. St. Bartholomew's tops Barbon behind the public house, the favourably titled Barbon Inn. The original foundations of the church are ancient and are marked on Speed's 1610 Map of Westmorland. The current structure is Austin and Paley designed with a foundation stone laid in 1892 by Blanche Marion, Lady Kay-Shuttleworth. I am not making these names up. The

church lych gate sets off the scene perfectly for the cameraman and model-village feel of Barbon. The gate is dedicated to the Reverend James Harrison for having a normal sounding name. No, I jest, he served 43 years in the parish, seeing the rebirth before his death in 1915 and it is a fitting memorial.

St. Bartholomew's is the first of the churches in the 'Rainbow Parish', briefly mentioned in the last chapter, and holds, as a result, a red flag. Holy Trinity, Casterton and St. John the Divine, Hutton Roof shine orange and yellow with the home church, the Church of St. Mary in Kirkby Lonsdale hoisting the green emblem. The spectrum is completed by All Saints at Lupton (blue), Holy Ghost at Middleton (indigo) and St. Peter at Mansergh (violet). Hubert James Austin and Edward Graham Paley provided the colour for many of the churches in the region and their distinctive gothic partnership with decorative and perpendicular fashion enables even the amateur observer to recognise an 'Austin and Paley' work.

Middleton, like Newbiggin before it, is a very common name throughout the country. One of the largest in the north being the relatively close-by and not-really-large-at-all, Middleton-in-Teesdale, which was made well known because of its connections to the Quaker-led London Lead Mining Company, but curiously also plays host to a River Lune. No other Middleton, or Newbiggin, is large and perhaps this is why they thrive ubiquitously. Here, Middleton stretches over many acres and is distinguished by no certain village centre.

It does, however, have plenty to commend it.

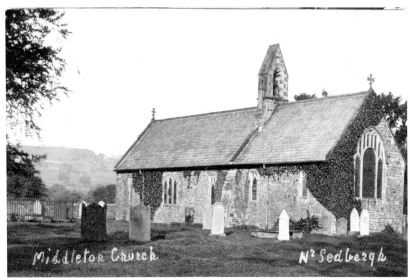

Middleton Church   N⁰ Sedbergh

The tourist will already have his eye fixed for influences from the field of religion; the praise of agriculture; tale of transport and pastime of pleasure. Middleton Hall is protected from the nearby lanes by an eighteen-foot high wall, yet this only serves to make the curious more curious.

Middleton Hall is associated with a famous sheep-clipping event from over two centuries ago. With the Bowness family in tenancy and the father of the family about to retire a massive clipping fair was arranged. Thirteen men brought over 2,000 sheep and 1,000 lambs from the fells. Seventy four-legged stools or creels were lined up for the occasion and the 'Middleton Ha' Clippin' was underway. Today it is a special treat for any child or adult alike to witness even a single shearing using the old fashioned clippers rather than the electric machine razor of the farmer cum barber. It must have been quite a sight, and sound, and smell; indeed, the atmosphere of the Lune landscape on that occasion would take the breath away today.

The Church of the Holy Ghost sits squarely against the road surrounded by farmland and a small car park welcomes careful drivers anticipant of the turning in. Its solo location somehow makes the church appear grander than those at Barbon and Casterton. Originally built in 1634 it, like its siblings, went through various modifications and restorations; firstly between 1812 and 1815, then again in 1879. The present church interior contains a record of the last reopening, with such detail as the Bishop allegedly having flu and an odd pictorial of a blind man with two right feet.

A Roman milestone from the Low Borrow to Over Borrow road has been re-erected near Middleton, at Hawking Hall, and marks, as an unessential guide, the 53rd mile from Carlisle. If today's visitor greets such a measurement with groans of anticlimax, just imagine how the marching Roman soldier would have felt with a considerable MPLIII miles (53 milia passuum) before reaching Luguvalium (Carlisle). Locals may say, 't'wad be a hefty lug' to Carlisle and they would not be wrong.

I would like to know how the Romans knew it was 53 miles! I would also like to know why we do not still use these straight roads as natural turnpikes today. I am told by my advisor and walking companion that it is simply a matter of maintenance and whilst the Roman Roads were fine in construction, they needed constant attention (much like today's!) and soon became water-bound, impassable and returned to nature very quickly if left unattended.

The Middleton milestone stands nearly six feet high and some way from the roadside, where parking is treacherous, and in the middle of a field so it is best not to expect access to be easy. Take the view from the roadside and I will let you know what else is chipped into the stonework, at least as it is told by my literary forbears. *Solo erutum restitut Gull Moore AD MDCCCXXXVI* can be translated as 'unearthed and restored by Gulliver Moore in 1836,' and was added by local clergyman Revd Dr. Linguard. An ancient cross, the

Standing Stone of Whelprigg is near this point too and while collecting stone monuments it is a good one to tick off.

It may be pure coincidence and highly likely to be a complete irrelevance but it is 52 miles from Forton to Penrith via the M6 motorway. I am also told that a Roman mile is different in length to our measurement today, whether that is in metric or in traditional pounds and shillings is unclear. If you say they must have had shorter legs then do not forget that they had walked all the way from Italy!

Just below Middleton is one of the few crossings available to road users at Rigmaden Bridge. A steel construction reminiscent of pontoon because of the name, which, to me, conjures up

wartime conflicts across the Netherlands. Indeed, the river appears to widen here as the valley floor makes a resistance to contour and fields plateau. Pools form inviting swimmers and fishermen to don trunks and cast rods.

This is also home to another sportsman, the canoeist. Rigmaden Bridge is a popular 'put-in' on the route down to Devil's Bridge. Signage appended to leaning trees dot the riverbank throughout the Lune and thankfully, most are visible directly from the bridges along the way. Signs vary from 'Canoeing' to 'No Canoeing', from information about which A.A. (Angling Association) owns the stretch, to signs long since

left blank to simply cause the wanderer to wonder and wander on.

In the autumn of 2003 a 'put-in' of a very different variety took place when some 65,000 baby salmon were released into the Lune as part of a joint initiative between the Middleton Hatchery Group and the Environment Agency. The fish, known as parr, were only six months old and a few inches long. They were released between Shap, Sedbergh and ten other sites along the Lune and its tributaries. In two years time they will have grown into smolts and will be ready for their oceanic journey.

The Lune runs parallel to the road here yet it is not always easy to see or gain access and the bridge crossings are always worthy contenders for the notebook. According to the Archdeacon of Richmond, of the Diocese of Chester, his wee Deanery of Lonsdale supports nineteen bridges across the Lune and her tributaries in Lonsdale Ward. Take your pad and collect Kirkby Lonsdale, Casterton, Barbon, Hodge, Blindbeck, Middleton Hall, Low and High Stockdale, New Bridge in Middleton, Old Bridge in Killington, Lincoln's Inn, Crook of Lune, Tarn Close, Beckfoot at Dillicar Smithy, Spittal, Lupton Mill, Tosca, New Keartswick, and Bleasbeck.

Lonsdale Ward is the smallest of the four 'Wards of Westmorland' at fourteen miles in length it only averages one and half miles in width for half of its length. As Middleton is left behind the options for the adventurer extend again and a varied choice of escape is possible. Back to Killington is the most common as the main road veers across that way. Another option is to head east for Sedbergh from beneath its belly.

DALES WAY

It was not intended for me to include a specific walk in my prose as this is covered in more detail in books dedicated to the rambler, hiker and climber; and now cyclist and no doubt the hang-glider, canoeist, pot-holer and sub-aqua diver. Indeed, the books are so specific now that each user of foot or pedal power can find the literature that best suits their age and ability. We have the choice and at the very least that is what we are continuously being told.

I am not sure if life is any easier with such a vast array of choices. Still, if one is able to step back and decide what role one wants to take then the selection starts to make itself. If on horseback it makes logical sense to use a book on bridleways. These are on the shelves yet rare and a better source will be dedicated internet sites. The same is true for those on bicycles (more accurately mountain bikes) or those wearing wet suits. No doubt the internet will provide guidelines for pogo stick users in years to come.

In 2003 there was an outbreak of cycle sign-posts across the region and plenty are to be seen intercepting footpaths, bridges and our narrow twisty roads. As if the very presence isn't con-fusing enough the signs look just like the normal road signs, except slightly smaller and invariably give lengthier distances between towns, presum-ably accounting for the cyclist's tendency to devi-ate along the route!

I put myself in a much simpler bracket than a deviating cyclist. I am a walker. I am not a long distance walker, although this depends on your definition of long distance. I am not a high peak walker, although this too depends on your defini-tion of hill, fell and or mountain. Regular walks of anything between five and fifteen miles suit me. Small peaks and valley floors where there are views - close and distant - and other attractions for my failing senses of sound and vision. This walk suits me and may suit you and offers enough Odd Corners to justify inclusion.

The Dales Way is not the only walking route in the district. We have already seen the Coast to Coast from Alfred Wainwright. There are plenty more options and many worth investigating. The Westmorland Heritage Walk is a valid addition as are the diverting walks that include other goals. For example, 'Walking down the Lune', 'Walking Roman Roads', 'Church Walks', 'Walking Old Railways' all help straighten your particular bend in the river. A comprehensive listing is given at the back of this book.

These and the Dales Way and the Coast to Coast can be done in manageable sections, and these sections need not be done in succession. You can

spend the rest of your life ticking them off and repeating the good ones. Indeed, the repeated walk is often the best as seasonal variations offer vastly different sights and scenes. If I mention the nettle then every shorts wearer will get my drift.

I am still not sure how to get the best out of the best book and what determines best is open to scrutiny. The book that details every blade of grass and wonky stile is out of date before it is published. Others take you five miles into a walk then expect you to field your own way home. Some provide just the right amount of guidance yet find themselves compiled in such a way that carriage is impractical. I often find that I attempt the walk first, by use of nose and Ordnance Survey map, and then refer in detail to my book sources on my return home. A mixture of personal experience, learned local knowledge (from learned locals) and plenty of source options works for me.

The Countryside Commission designated the Dales Way a 'recreational footpath.' It is an interesting term. This year the rugged sister landscape of the North Pennines (in particular High Force and High Cup Nick) has been awarded 'geopark' status. Apparently a geopark is the equivalent of a World Heritage Site status on a par with the Taj Mahal and the Grand Canyon. Geoparks are a global extension of our own Areas of Outstanding Natural Beauty. You will probably know them as AONBs of which there are 41 in England and Wales.

The first AONB designation was made in 1956 (The Gower). It was not until July 1959 that the commission considered proposals for Howgill Fell AONB status together with the adjacent Silverdale region. Typically, I suspect, no decision was made and even after further meetings in October 1959, November 1959, March 1960 and October 1960 decisions were deferred.

In June 1961 a commission party visited the Howgill and Silverdale areas. The result was more indecision as our Howgill Fells had become linked to the designation of the North Pennines (now a geopark!) and uncertainty had arisen with regards differentiation between AONB and national park (which as we know was granted in 1954 in the realisation of the Yorkshire Dales National Park).

The North Pennines was granted AONB status in 1988. I will confuse the situation by adding that English Heritage's National Mapping programme surveyed the Howgill Fells between 1992 and 1994. For once the Howgills were high up in the pecking order only being behind the Yorkshire Dales, Dartmoor, Kent, Thames Valley and Hertfordshire in the programme. This may not seem too great an honour but it is relevant when areas such as the Cotswolds and Cornwall are still under survey. We should also remember that Britain has been the world's best-mapped nation since King George III founded Ordnance Survey. So, I am pleased for the area that we are recognised as beautiful and that the footpath is for recreation. Geoparks have been with us since 2000 and I can only guess the name will grow on us.

Back to the Dales Way which is a very popular route linking the West Riding of Yorkshire with the Lake District. Totalling about 75 miles and the whole lot can be walked in one week in relatively easy stages and starts beside the 'Old Bridge' over the River Wharfe at Ilkley. It finishes at Bowness and this can be somewhat of a culture shock, as although Bowness is a very beauti-

ful little town, it unfortunately mirrors Keswick for tourist-mania and, as you know, I feel uncomfortable in such company. The Howgill section of the Dales Way is marvellous and explores many distracting avenues to suit the exploring rambling type, who may consider him, or her, open to simple pleasures.

Dent to Grayrigg (or Grayrigg to Dent) can be done in one day, yet the observant walker may want to take a more leisurely outlook and split into sections. The typical guidebook will give

plenty of options for start and end points (or end pints, as rambler's refreshment is often an accepted prize for such endeavours).

The Dales Way is well marked although this does not guarantee an easy passage even with nettles taken out of the equation. As soon as you walk across a field path with hesitation the caretaker principle is bound to come into play. Bear with me on this diversion. Normally notorious by their absence, i.e. when needed, there are certain occupations that match the caretaker principle.

Let me explain. If, as kids, we were ever on school grounds without permission, then who would appear round the quietest of corners but the school caretaker. If a game of cricket was to be enjoyed on the periphery of the cricket square yet the ball rolled under the guarding rope and onto the hallowed wicket, as soon as the wire was crossed, the groundsman would appear from behind a tree. Even in innocence guilt would be implied. Traffic wardens are only ever seen when you are looking for a space and even when legally parked the tendency is to worry that his small print is different to those stated on the meter.

The same principle applies when pausing on a field path. Out pops the farmer. Open enquiry will follow in a manner to put the footman in their position. 'Dusta knaa wherst ya garn?' It would

The walk circumnavigates the bottom side of Sedbergh and takes the walker from Millthrop Bridge through to the disused mill at Birks. This short section of under a mile is a pleasant diversion from Sedbergh itself and will suit those not wanting to do anything more than an extended outer lap of Sedbergh. It's a nice little route for children too and offers good views across to Sedbergh School.

The next stage follows the Rawthey, bypasses Brigflatts Quaker Meeting House (so, don't think you can just 'pop-in'), joins half-a-mile of busy road, and then

be too arrogant to answer with a strong affirmative 'Yes, thank you'. The question was posed so that you would have to ask for confirmatory assistance. 'We think so, are we right for Low Branthwaite?' Any resulting conversation is again with a mood of reluctance and power and positioning.

Faced with such obstacles we can feel uneasy before and during such soft contretemps, yet afterwards a knowing nod to 'caretaker principle' sees us happily on our way. Watch out for a subtler approach such as 'Thaas dun weil ta get thee here', or the pessimistic encouragement of 'thaad bitta crack on, tis ganna git thee wet afore lang', and two years post foot and mouth we still hear 'did thee disinfect thaa boots?' It makes the challenge of nettles a triviality. And of course, the custodian of the countryside is usually right with his forecast of inclemency so you would be advised to take heed of his weather warning.

twists back on itself to head north past Luneside farm and to Lincoln's Inn Bridge. Many will greet Lincoln's Inn Bridge with a sigh and 'oh, we are here' as this is where the Sedbergh road crosses the Lune to and from the M6. Conversation will turn to enquiry about the name Lincoln's Inn and great theories about highflying legal connections, Lincoln's Inn being one of four legal societies of London that make up the Inns of Court. It may be a disappointment to discover that the name is a simple recognition of the fact that the farmhouse, once an Inn, used to be owned by a chap called Lincoln.

Joyce Scobie, in *Bridges of Sedbergh, Garsdale and Dent* (for the Sedbergh and District History Society), informs us that Lincoln's Inn Bridge was damaged in the Civil War and previously went by the name of Crowder Bridge. She also refers to the 1752 survey of local bridges and reports that the bridge was maintained up to one side by the West Riding of Yorkshire and up to the other by Westmorland, the river clearly making a logical county boundary. The division also meant that the repair and upkeep of the bridge may not always have been as it should.

I mention this as a tip to travellers wanting something to add to their 'I-spy' list on jolly jaunts out and about. Watch out, when crossing a county boundary, to see if there is any change in quality or style with the road surface and sur-roundings. You may find white lines on sticky tar-mac coming abruptly to a halt and meeting a flaky crumbly bumpy road on the 'other side'. It is good measure of proficiency and prosperity, or of poor productivity and poverty.

It may suit to leave the Dales Way here and head back to Sedbergh and this circular route offers a slightly larger variation on the Birks circuit. However, you may rue the opportunity not to bag a couple more miles as the next section of the route goes right under the disused railway viaduct with Firbank and Whinney Haw behind. The unusual structure of the bridge with the metal frame in the middle makes the camera an essential part of the rambler's rucksack. He or she will be even more grateful for remembering the camera as along the next few miles the footpath offers moments to pause at every stile and gate as the countryside loses that barren feeling of the open and typical Dales moorland to become lush and warm and comforting. The fields, the trees, the streams, the farmhouses, the dry stonewalls and the ancient hedges, the tighter valley. It just makes me smile. Faced with a world of choices, this stroll out is not a bad one and some days it is difficult to call a halt to the walk and return to base.

BRIGGFLATTS MEETING HOUSE

As we have seen, the rise of non-conformity in the region led many people to abandon the older church ways and set up new sects. As 'Seekers' they had to hold their meetings in private homes and barns, such was the speed at which they developed. In some way this essential simplicity must have also influenced their values and to this day meetings of the Quakers are still held in what are known as 'Meeting Houses'. In the 18th century, John Wesley's Methodist followers and other fragmented movements such as George Whitefield's Calvinists, grew in favour across Yorkshire and the homes and barns simply became too full to hold the needs of the mining and farming families.

Chapels were born and often built without a dedicated, experienced architect, and erected simply by the efforts of the hard labour of the local

workforce. This immediately conjures a cinematic image of a vast celebration of people with picnics and parties. I wonder.

As congregations grew in strength and resources the chapels became architect designed and very much what we understand today as being 'designer'. Deliberately unique and alien to the recognised residential nature of the houses these buildings adopted church styles and the chapel was born. The Meeting House of the Quakers is different in that it has never quite bowed to the evolution seen in chapel architecture. This is seen by a purposeful effort to think inwardly rather than allow too much influence from the outside. In other words the simple principles of Quakerism did not allow deviation from the path.

Rufus Jones explained the spirituality by placing an immediate awareness of God through their 'inner life' rather than a God conceived 'up there'. He summed up the ethic by stating that 'religion does not rise outside and flow in; it springs up inside and flows out.' George H Gorman in his standard Quaker textbook *Introducing Quakers* (1969) takes the concept even further and brilliantly describes the indescribable:

We struggle to find words to describe that of which we are aware, and they evade us, because no words are fully adequate to express a state that defies definition. Perhaps the words 'life', 'spirit' and 'consciousness' are among those that come most readily to our aid, but even they fail to disclose the full sense of our identity as living beings. Our first reaction to our interior journey may well be one of anxiety, or even of terror, as we sense our insignificance, finitude and loneliness. But as we allow ourselves to be calmed by the stillness at the centre of our being, we can find a deeper awareness of our rootedness in life itself, and of our relatedness to other people. We know that it is from this deep place that insights into the real meaning of life arise, and the power to live it is found. In this kind of dynamic, vital experience we realise that we have discovered a new level of existence, in which our spirit is fused with spirit itself in a creative encounter.

If the Quaker message first came down from the fells in 1652 it may seem like it took a long time before someone like Gorman could put the message into words; except that the message was there from the start and part of the Quaker ethic has been to put work into keeping it there. In many respects this is why the shape and form of the meeting houses remains unchanged. The effort for change is to be made internally, by the individual.

Of course, as a group of reformers they had to work hard and nor did they want or need to 'change the world.' Briggflatts was often at the heart of conference as conformity was challenged. And here by 'conformity' I mean the Quaker conformity, or 'traditions'. The format of the Quaker Meeting was and is essential to appreciation and understanding of these goals. Recognising that it takes personal effort to grow along spiritual lines, and not playing lip service to attending meetings, many 18th century meetings would have ministers declare from Amos 6:1 'Woe to those who are at ease in Zion.' Disciplined traditions, held by a core group of elders determined the uniformity.

Quaker meetings are focused affairs where

silence is considered a virtue as it accentuates the mood of communion and empathy for internal exploration. Early Friends used the term 'centring down' and in some ways it is a form of meditation aimed at heightening awareness. It is undoubtedly an experience where emotional intensity is increased by the unity of the group. A modern way to comprehend the feeling is to understand the excitement and fervour of being in a football crowd of 50,000 fans rather than a

land bought for the use as a burial ground to serve the 'Friends of Sedbergh, Dent, Garsdale, Middleton, Killington and Ewbank.' Being described as three falls of land (a fall being one pole, or thirty square yards) more land was added in 1674 at the corner of a close in Little Briggflatts.

Additions and alterations to floors and galleries took place throughout the 18th century but none radical enough to alter the architectural form of the original design. Likewise in the 20th century the panelling and balustrades were repaired and renewed within keeping with the original fashion. The most significant change was the building of a bathroom in 1964.

The uniqueness of the interior is seen in the lofted galleries taking a horseshoe shape around three sides backing on to the blank walls where only the south face of the building is home to a door and windows. One of the greatest novelties of the earliest house was that Cumberland stone was used for the roof, instead of thatch. This gave it stability but little weather proofing and with an earthen floor it must seem positively luxurious today.

Some local relics still remain and part of the old stone market cross from Sedbergh now stands on its own plinth in the grounds of Briggflatts. The plinth informs the visitor that the cross was part of the market from 1550 to 1854. The plinth is nearly 150 years old and will deserve its own place on a new plinth soon. Then again, the principles seen at Briggflatts are not about new physical entities,

dispirited group of only fifty, or more profoundly to be at a funeral where sadness prevails and overwhelms simply because of the intense 'group' emotion in the congregation.

When words are eventually spoken in these Quaker assemblies it makes them all the more powerful and profound. The setting of the room is as important as the silence and this is where the Quaker Meeting House comes into its own. The seats may be benches in older rooms or simple chairs in the newer ones and these arranged in a circle, or square, with a table in a hollow centre. There are no pulpits or altars, no liturgy and no hymns.

Briggflatts Meeting House is the oldest such meeting house in the north and has a history like no other. It is easily missed from the main road from Kendal to Sedbergh and drivers going too fast, as most sadly do along this stretch, will miss the turning altogether. It began life as a piece of these are considered an interruption to the simplicity of inner observation and it is within that sphere that change is considered essential.

Eastern and western religions in a converging world deliver modern reform in a new light. New non-conformism and reform still concerns the spiritual and matters of the soul. The region once again takes a lead. You only have to look in *Sedbergh & District Lookaround* to see where it is heading. June Parker runs an acupuncture clinic in Sedbergh and often features in *Lookaround* with commentaries on 'chee' and cycles of nature aimed at ridding our body of cravings for coffee, cigarettes and chocolate. June alerts us to methods to allow our bodies to trust in themselves and make its needs known. Of course, to do this is not easy at first as the draw for impulse and 'quick-fix' is very powerful indeed.

Being a convert myself to energy therapies I too can wax lyrical about the subject and, trust me, it is relevant to my point on Quaker reform. Acupuncture pre-dates the Quaker way by some considerable time having started in Tibet around 4000BC. Yet the Westerner only began to 'see the light' in the 1960s. The principles of acupuncture derive from the meridian, or energy system of the body, which is a series of channels or pathways running from the feet to the face and the face to the hands transporting vital energy.

The meridian system is responsible for the distribution of energy or chee (Qi or chi) throughout the body thus nourishing and influencing body, mind and spirit. There are many ways to introduce aspects of chee into your consciousness and meditation remains one of the most accessible. Meditation is something that must be practiced to be able to do it well. Indeed, it must be done 'religiously'. The Quaker service of sitting in silence may be closer to 'reflection' than meditation yet parallels must be drawn and within that simple ethic of inner peace we can mirror these two reformations bridged by 350 years.

Auricular acupuncture combined with meditation focuses on energising organs concerned with cleansing the body i.e. liver, lungs and kidneys, and points that calm the emotions (Shenmen points). Needles are not always necessary. Simple tugging around your ears, gently pulling and massaging the lobes for a few minutes stimulates the acupuncture points opening up the electromagnetic reservoirs on the skin and releasing

your energies for the day. Get yourselves along to a Quaker meeting and observe how many ears are being rubbed.

Change within the health care field comes most readily from its professionals who identify new trends and see the need for establishing credible practice in a new direction. Such themes can be managed on a domestic level too and it gives me tremendous pleasure to see Howgill folk at the forefront of the growing field of energy psychology. How better is this summed up but in the expanding discipline of Neuro-Linguistic Programming (known to all as NLP, of course) which was developed in America in the early 70s from studying the thinking and behavioural skills used by particularly effective and successful people.

One of the founders, Robert Dilts focused on the need for personal change and defined 'identity' as the most important value to the individual. Within the value he described identity as 'my basic sense of self, my core values and my mission in life.' NLP is used in energy medicine to help individuals, and groups, with 'lost identity' where the person has little or no sense of 'self'. The great power and strength of the Howgillian identity is littered throughout the pages of this book.

SEDBERGH

Sedbergh, Sedburgh, Sedberwe, Sadborourgh, Sadber, Sedber - all of which are met with in manuscript or printed matter - show a reasonable amount of elasticity in the form of the name; and even Sebber- the ultimate residuum of indolent articulation- is occasionally heard from native lips... I can only plead in my desire to establish three things, which are not usually present to every one's mind at the same time; that the name of our little town should be Sedbergh to the eye, Sedber to the ear, and Sadda's bergh, or hill-fort, to the understanding W Thompson, Sedbergh, Garsdale and Dent, 1892

Sedbergh says Dr. Eilert Ekwall is a common name in Scandanavia meaning a flat-topped hill. Whether the doctor's own names of Eilert and Ekwall are as common will remain a mystery.

Another derivation is 'Sadda's Berg' where Sadda had his fort, one supposes on the flat-topped hill. The town centre of Sedbergh thankfully forces every driver to slow down. A complex road system (it's only complex on the first visit) and a cobbled one-way main street make a steady wheel a necessity. With two car parks to choose from it is easily to feel annoyed when paying for parking in the higher one only to walk around the town to discover the lower park is free.

St. Andrew's Church stands down from the main houses and at first glance doesn't appear as large as it really is and the tendency for the pedestrian is to head for the shops and tea rooms of the main street. St. Andrews has been placed in a corner many times as the borders of church elders have each taken a turn in being head office, well, deputy head office. The Archdiocese of York handed Sedbergh to Chester, and on to Ripon and today as part of the Bradford Diocese, albeit now in Cumbria.

George Fox is famously drawn preaching beneath a yew tree and part of that same yew sits displayed on a southern window sill having taken a journey from its place in the ground (near the grave of Canon Platt), to a home at Briggflatts Meeting House and then back to St. Andrews.

Sedbergh sometimes reminds me of one of the Greek island towns of say, Skiathos or Skopelos, where the streets duck and dive behind the main avenue, itself narrow and tight. Flower baskets swing above whitewashed steps and old men sit four to a bench smoking and stuttering and sometimes smiling. Women paddle about with work to do and fluffy cats sit high observing the daily routine of timeless traditions. Absent youth departed for urban opportunity. The cheery comfort of everyone knowing everyone else's business and the appreciating need for tourism as the ticket for survival consolidates the comparison. A little idyllic perhaps, yet shared ideals leave the only contrast to the sunlight.

Sedbergh's freedom is realised in the most peculiar of observations. The public toilet at the foot of Joss Lane is open 24 hours a day. A sad indictment of our times that this lavatorial facility should be so rare. At least those needing relief 'after hours' know where to go. An odd corner and an odd convenience.

There are plans to change the commercial dynamics of Sedbergh and make it into a book

MILLTHROP BRIDGE SEDBERGH

outstretched stomach tells of my appreciation and I struggle to resist the Wensleydale sausage, the Dentdale sausage, the Ravenstonedale Red, the Dalesman, the Sunshine sausage, the Jubilee, the Karoowors, the Oriental Pork and Cashew, and another ten or so traditional varieties.

The book town plan moved on a pace in 2003 and a strategy document was made available for anyone taking an interest. It does tend to focus on the market of second hand books rather than promoting the good work done in many excellent new books (well, I would say that). To boost interest further the town's organising types have also promoted a book boot. Along the lines of a typical 'car boot' sale where prospective sellers expose their wares,

town like Hay-on-Wye or Wigtown. I think this is a brilliant idea. Well, I like books. Collecting, reading, touching, admiring, writing, giving.

I may not be so much in favour if the theme was to be perfumery or haberdashery. If books fail to bind the town another option would certainly not be butchery. There would be little competition to rank by Steadmans and their speciality sausage. I would not normally be one to take note of their registration approval with the Guild of Q Butchers or their EN45004 inspection standard or their Assured British Meat Certificate of Conformity; I would simply taste the sausage. It is only through researching this book have I discovered the technical standard of their business and I can't help but notice that their sausage is 'conforming.' In other words, my

MAIN STREET, SEDBERGH.

and solely books, in the Joss Street car park every Wednesday.

I was there to witness the first attempt on Wednesday 28 May 2003. Two keen stallholders turned up. Out of small acorns grow large oaks, and slowly too as the next week the book boot was cancelled because of a legal hitch in market rights. A subsequent week brought rain by the bucket load and books remained boot bound. The cascade continued however and while not as big as perhaps hoped the book boot doggedly continues and is gaining in popularity.

The next stage sees plans for vacant buildings to be turned into multiple units of varying sizes. This will allow a flexible and versatile option to book sales from the casual trader who may want to offer only a bookcase of around a hundred

Main Street, Sedbergh.

books to the semi-professional who can keep a whole corner fully stocked. You can't keep book men (and women) down and I hope and expect the future of the book town to be one of prosperity.

The name for the first shared bookshop is the Sleepy Elephant, in recognition of Alfred Wainwright's elephantine analogy. Hopefully, it is a name people will not forget. It opened in the first week of September 2003. Next is the major unit in the main street that will, hopefully, be turned into a huge menagerie of book corners and specialist galleries. The prospects for the town are astounding and already new shops and amenities are being attracted to the town. We already see the main street 'bookended' by Fraser Gardiner's interesting Reflections at one end and the very Fine Art Gallery at the other. Steady does it Sedbergh.

Wire Bridge, Sedbergh.

I like the simplicity of Sedbergh. Almost too simple and perhaps a strange word to describe a town whose life and subsistence depends on the school, which famously produces scholars and sportsmen of world renowned. Sir John Otway, Viscount Lonsdale, George Fleming, John Fothergill, Adam Sedgwick, Hartley Coleridge and John Inman, the compiler of tide tables, all took lessons from Sedbergh School.

Founded in 1523 the school has always poked its head above the parapet of its neighbours and not cared to look down on them. I played for the great Appleby Grammar School rugby fifteen of the late 70s, a team that commanded most of Cumbria and indeed represented the county at Air Training Corps national level defeating Ireland and then London and the south east. Sedbergh were still a cut above and a class above. As such, we were never invited to play them.

It is a school that has no doubt for its comparative size produced the greatest number of rugby internationals, famously England and Lions captain Will Carling. And now, Will Greenwood who played for England against Australia in the most dramatic of World Cup Finals in November 2003 when England won 20-17. Both players encapsulating meritous drive and determination.

Their attitude has to be admired and whilst not with the same aggression and intimidation as the All Blacks' song and dance (sic.) the 'Haka', the Sedberghians have a rugby song, which commands due respect and loyalty to their home:

> *The sunshine is melting the snow on the Calf,*
> *And the Rawthey is loud in the dale,*
> *And there seems every chance of our getting a 'half',*
> *If the weather glass tells a true tale.*
> *What shall we do with it? Suck lollipops?*
> *Swelter and sicken till tea?*
> *Loaf in the town and lounge in the shops?*
> *Waste money and muscle? Not we!*
> *Play up, bonnie Browns, for House and Cup*
> *For the fame of the school play up!*
> *Never say die, make it a try,*
> *Carry it through to the goal line!*

Our Appleby team did get to play Kirkby Lonsdale Grammar. I collected lists, records and anecdotes even then. We beat them 23 points to 6 on 23 March 1977; I played left wing. At

Appleby our singing was less rounded and more raucous. Apparently, there is an Appleby school song, but our rugby days were only likely to offer choral reprises of *When the cow kicked Nellie, in the belly, in the barn.* Sedbergh School has good right to feel proud.

The fell path above the school and down to Cautley hosts the first half of the annual Wilson Race as part of Sedbergh School's traditions. Held on the Tuesday nearest Lady's Day in March the boys take a ten-mile run from the school up Howgill Lane and over the top set off by the chimes of three bells from the church clock. The race is named after Bernard Wilson and first set boys away in 1881.

The current record for the race is held by Charles L. Sykes who ran it in 1993 with a time of one hour eight minutes and four seconds. The record had stood for 94 years, being held by C. E. Pumphrey, who, for his day, must have been an outstanding athlete. The course has apparently

remained relatively unaltered during this time whereas fitness ideals and training techniques have not; perhaps there is merit at rekindling the fresh-air attitude and fell life that Pumphrey clearly exhibited. Not all records can be rewarded via the gym.

The run follows the contour line 100 feet above the River Rawthey before crossing it at Wardses and up onto West Baugh Fell above Cocks Dub. I went to watch the Wilson Run of 2003. Of the 40 boys (and with a handful of Lupton girls giving equal effort - another measure of the 'modern' times) a lad called Hoggy was in the lead at the Wardses Bridge

Sedbergh School, Sedbergh, Yorkshire. Cricket Field and Winder.

runners completed the course except for one sprained ankle. Holmes ran a beautifully steady race, his long steady strides gaining him an invaluable lead across the heather. Under the conditions his time of 1'16'8 must rank among the best times for several years. Phillips alone might have made the race an extremely close thing for he was much faster than Holmes on the road but a stitch at Hebblethwaite made the issue almost certain. Beaven looked very competent and untroubled when he came in and both he and Hele ran smoothly and sensibly. The most conspicuous effort in the race was Cavaghan's. Had he chosen to let Holmes and Phillips go their own way unchallenged he might well have made himself a safe third but he ran

six-mile mark. The effort was as uplifting as the roadside support from parents and onlookers. Incidentally, the houses are Evans, Hart, Lupton, Powell, School, Sedgwick and Winder, each having around 55 pupils, although the Lupton girls have risen to 80. Numbers are increasing so rapidly that Robertson, a second girls' house, opened in 2003.

While later researching Sedbergh and Wilson I discovered a 60-year-old copy of *The Sedberghian* from 1943. The Wilson report makes entertaining reading:

It is impossible to cite all those who ran well. Considering the weather it was remarkable that 75% of the competition completed the course under 1'30'0. Many people took nasty falls but all the

long duels with both of them before falling back outrun at the top of Danny. The result was that he had to try and fight off Beaven and Hele in an exhausted condition, two gruelling and unsuccessful struggles which he nevertheless survived to finish a very courageous fifth.

The journal has many interesting articles and anecdotes curious for today. The report from the Sedgwick Society apologises for a decrease in the number of lectures and films because of the 'great increase in time which both masters and boys have had to devote to wartime activities' and follows this with thanks to a Mr Hogg for his lecture on Iraq. It would be a nice thought to suppose that Mr Hogg was a relative of Hoggy from 2003, who under his proper title of J. Hogg, Powell House, was in the pink with a winning time of one hour sixteen minutes and forty-one seconds.

CAUTLEY SPOUT AND RAWTHEY BRIDGE

Cautley Spout tumbles 700 feet in a series of white water cascades and rains relentlessly in its own odd corner shadowed by Brant Fell and Yarlside. In the fields below Cautley Spout is a plaque on a raised plinth. It gives a short history lesson and tells the passer-by that stone-age man used to have a settlement in this valley floor.

A path ran from the camp to the foot of the falls and then stopped. It supposes that the falls had a special significance to the pre-millennial settlers, but does not take a guess at what that might be. Is worship a natural assumption? Today's path is well laid and well used. In 2,000 years time will our descendant's discover this path and suppose a special significance too? Will they make the comment that tourism is the natural assumption?

At the waterfall, the path takes the steepest incline where steady boots and a steady mind are required. Instructions are signed to keep the walker on one side of a rope as part of an erosion control process. The walker, now feeling effort in his or her knees, is asked to vary his route and zig-zag. Hopeful demands. This will not make any difference. The tourist is relentless. And so is nature.

Readers will not be surprised to find another sheepfold by Andy Goldsworthy at Cautley. Red Gill is in another style and unveiled as a Washfold. This large sheepfold has a built-in cairn and celebrates sheep farming renewal. Whether directly as a result of the horrors of foot and mouth in 2001 or indirectly laid out as a memorial to the culture of agronomics, once again its art form and message is deliberately left open to scrutiny.

A great deal of bitterness and emotional confusion still hangs in the air regarding the consequences of foot and mouth in the area and people are still sensitive, with very few not having a strong opinion on the management and outcomes of the tragedy. I congratulate Andy Goldsworthy in offering this as some of form of cleansing in symbolic form, even though it is open to gratuitous misinterpretation.

Built in 1600s as the farmhouse High Haygarth (Low Haygarth is by the roadside a few hundred yards to the south) the Cross Keys was first extended in the early 1700s. Quakers John and Agnes Howgill were its keepers until it became an inn in the late 1700s when the old road over Bluecaster was closed and the turnpike down the line of the River Rawthey was built. The building has a deathly secret. Dorothy Benson, herself a Quaker, is buried underneath the dining room, although for obvious reasons this fact is not advertised too loudly.

The intention would not have been to place her beneath the diners as in the time of her burial the area was part of the garden. Dorothy was the first wife of Colonel Gervase Benson, Mayor of Kendal and ally to Cromwell. As a supporter of the Westmorland Seekers he became influenced by George Fox, meeting him at Briggflatts and High Haygarth.

Dorothy was also clearly influenced to the extent of landing herself in York gaol for heckling a priest. She only to survived prison for a couple of years and, out of respect to her driven and passionate life, her husband brought her back to Haygarth to be buried.

More extensions to the property were seen in the 19th century and through various quirks of fate the inn became temperance in 1902. It was left to the National Trust in 1949 on condition it kept its temperance qualities as requested via the will of former owner A. E. Bunney. Run to the highest and friendliest standards possible, Alan and Chris Clowes play host today to a very special corner of the Howgills. If the inside of the Cross Keys is closed or holding a private function then gasping ramblers can avail themselves of refreshment round the back which usually remains open for outdoor imbibitions.

David Boulton, in his excellent book *Early Friends in Dent* (1986), discusses at length the

155

efforts made by Gervase Benson to publicise, promote and publish the *Truth*. Benson, a 'busy pamphleteer' recognised a certain frustration in the surrounds of Sedbergh and exclaimed that, 'Sedbergh has become an unruly place. The number of Alehouses are great, no less than fourteen in a little town... the priest of the place a common frequenter of them.'

The local issues aside, Benson appears to be the first Quaker to make a stand in London having visited there in November 1653. It is supposed by Boulton that Benson's observations prompted the Quaker executive at Swarthmoor to publish *Truth* and prompt the missionary work of the Valiant Sixty. Separated by many years it is fascinating to read both Benson's and Boulton's accounts of the social dynamics between the unlikely twins of Sedbergh and Dent. This is not the place to diversify on such traits, but I will certainly be observing any differences on my future travels.

Whilst on the veranda of the Cross Keys, opportunity should arrive to take consideration, not only of the marvellous view but also of the validity of inscription on the said veranda, penned by William Blake and stating 'Great things are done when men and mountains meet. These are not done by jostling in the street'. And then inevitably moving on to discourses such as the origins of the River Rawthey (the 'river of the red one') and the difference between an inn, an alehouse, a tavern, and a good old pub.

With astonishing appropriateness this is a conversation I shall continue on these pages. The public house or 'pub' is a relatively modern term of Victorian origin. We have to thank our old friends the Romans for introducing us to drinking houses. Roman settlements would have 'tabernae' which would offer food and wine (presumably after the luxury of a bathhouse experience). The departure of the Romans saw the loss of the tabernae too.

Much later, during the 12th century, when trade and travel took off there became a need for houses that could provide hospitality in the guise of food and overnight accommodation. Largely run and controlled by the monasteries, the inn was born. Again, after a gap of some 400 years, the social dynamics of our country changed as urban life prospered. This saw the birth of the tavern and the alehouse. Taverns, largely selling

only wine, were for the professional classes to embrace a mix of business and pleasure, whereas the alehouse was a shelter and lesser establishment for the poorer classes.

Then comes our connection. The Civil War, which began in 1642, was observed by the Puritans as an excuse for much of the country split in their allegiance between Parliament and the King, yet free from any duty to battle, to escape the politics by hiding in the numerous alehouses that were ready to capture a keen market.

The non-drinking groups were born with the non-conformists. At the same time three new drinks were about to bring radical change to the drinking habits of the nation.

Coffee was introduced in 1650, chocolate in 1657 and tea in 1660. The English have been traditionally associated with tea, yet we were the first European country to offer coffee commercially (and it was us who introduced it to America). The first official coffee house was in St. Michael's Alley, Cornhill, London and opened its doors in George Fox's year of 1652.

I am indebted to The Bramah Museum, London (the world's first museum devoted to tea and coffee) for more interesting digressions. By 1670 coffee houses were everywhere and were the trendy bars that, in some respects, mirror the high street fashion of today. As the centres of gossip and speculation, some of which was written down and circulated, it is claimed that newspapers began in the coffee houses. When the mixture of business and pleasure necessitated quiet corner alcoves coffee houses began insisting on a small contribution being made in a box to secure privacy. This collecting vessel was marked 'to insure prompt service' and another British invention 'TIPS' were born.

In 1674 outraged women, angry that husbands were spending too much time in the coffee houses issued the 'Women's Petition Against Coffee' listing the following dissatisfaction: '...coffee leads men to trifle away their time, scald their chops, and spend their money, all for a little base, black thick, nasty, bitter, stinking nauseous puddle water...'

Temperance came into being much later and again finds harmony with the Howgill story and relates to Richard Herd's essay on Free Trade. The temperance movement epitomised Victorian values and was influenced by both evangelicalism and utilitarianism. The first period of the

23833. Cautley Craggs, Sedbergh.   F. Frith & Co., Ltd.

side of course. Masons, in the employ of the church for construction of church buildings, were also making stone bridges to replace the timber ones. With this knowledge it is plain to see why they are often discussed with ecclesiastical fashion and admired from a spiritual viewpoint. One could argue that there is a psychological mind-game at play here with the church building tempting some sort of salvation and the bridge offering a simple, but desired, safe passage. The late great Arthur Raistrick captures the development of the stone bridge better than anyone in his 1976 booklet, *Buildings in the Yorkshire Dales*:

In the first 50 years of the 17th century nearly all Dales bridges were repaired or rebuilt in stone on the site of earlier bridges of timber... The 17th century work and some that is earlier is to be seen in most of the bridges if it is looked for underneath; the old narrow arch is often incorporated in the present wider bridge and the older ones are usually built on ribs. The newer arch is often flatter than the old one. On the older portions it is common to find masons marks, principally on the piers and on the finer tooled soffit stones of the arches. On a single bridge there is often a moderate variety, ten or a dozen different marks being found. These marks identify the work of different masons who did the stone dressing and shaping and enabled the master mason to keep a check on the work of his men and the quarry banker hands.

temperance movement aimed to control drunkenness rather than abolish alcohol. The Beer Act of 1830 allowed free trade of beer and it was thought that freely available beer would reduce the consumption of gin, which was seen as more harmful. It became clear that beer could be equally intoxicating and in 1832 the call for an alcohol-free society led to the common term for temperance types as "teetotallers'. It can be misleading, as temperance does not necessarily mean abstinence. Whatever your pleasure...

Running through the Cautley district the land distinctly, at least to the experienced eye, turns once more into Westmorland mode from its busier Yorkshire tightness. By now readers should have picked up on my love for bridges. Whether this be due to their architectural aspect or their humanist analogy of providing a helping hand to man, it does not matter. I like them.

Piety was the reason for building bridges in monastic times, apart from getting to the other

In addition to the familiar packhorse and

clapper bridges there are others around the north west of England that bear their name in relation to their function. For example, stock bridges near fulling-mills or 'stocks', and sepulchre bridges for ritualistic passage of the funeral party. The perception that the majority of bridges were rapidly turned into the packhorse style is not exactly true as skilled labour was required and as such many bridges remained as wood. These wooden bridges, typically stang bridges, were at greater risk from the elements and prone to damage due to high water as well as the natural wear and tear of supporting heavier carriage traffic. However, their durability was still substantial compared with today's 'build-them-and-run' varieties.

Collingwood in his CWAAS discourse about bridges (Transactions 1927) compliments Sweet Bridge, a mile north of Grayrigg on the Whinfell road, as being 'decayed' in 1692 yet surviving another 200 years before being washed away in a flood. With water levels occasionally reaching unexpected levels, even the bridges had to have their own flood escape tunnels and diversions for the unforgiving waters that sweep down the fells and ultimately man can have no answers. Of course, bridges were often to be used for foot and high water use alone when fords were in more common usage. Even now, some fourteen fords are marked on the Ordnance Survey map within a one mile radius of the Cross Keys Hotel.

Rawthey Bridge certainly fits our description of belonging to an odd corner. It has had a chequered history, which is recorded as gaining royal interest some 500 years ago. On 20 March 1584/5, Queen Elizabeth issued a commission to Robert Tempest and seven other esquires of the counties of York and Westmorland to 'enquire about the late fall of Rawthey Bridge, and to take measures for the rebuilding of the same.'

On 13 April the following year, Richard Dudley wrote that he could not meet the commissioners on the 26th instant for he had a horse to run that day in the race at Langwathby. The matter rested for a year. This immediately recalls the speed and urgency at which the Countryside Commission sprung into action when considering the Howgills as an AONB in the last century. Then the Earl of Huntingdon wrote again to Robert Tempest, on 5 May 1586, saying that her majesty's subjects were much troubled for want of repair of Rawthey Bridge.

On 12 September, the Queen and her council wrote yet again to Tempest, saying that she 'marvels at their negligence in the execution of her former orders concerning the rebuilding of Rawthey Bridge, and straightly commands them to meet at Sedbergh on the 7 or 8 October in order to take measure in the matter and make certificate of their proceedings before the 20 May next.' The bridge appears on a list of public bridges made on 28 April 1679. As we have seen before, bridges have a limited life span and in 1820 a new bridge with a stunning single arch rising seventeen feet with a span of 34 feet was built 50 yards below the decayed one.

The bridge is granted its odd corner status by, not only being on a significant corner, but by possessing an interesting carving of a face in the stonework on the eastern side. There are two schools of thought as to whom the face belongs. One suggests a child, and that the child may have a friend on another stone which has been lost to the river years ago. There is a space in the bridge wall for this second child. These two children are said to have befriended the masons and workmen during the bridge construction. The tale goes that they 'plied the bridge-builders with tea.'

Another story gaining in popularity is that the head belongs to a young woman in the manner of Jill McBain who was kind to the builders. Whether her favours were limited to brewing tea is open to speculation but with simple beverages as our theme for this piece it is refreshing to the tone to infuse her character with purity and moderation.

BLUECASTER

To me, the name Bluecaster hints of a speciality cheese from Lancashire and no doubt to others around the world it will suggest many very different things. Early references are few. Over a century ago W. Thompson in *Sedbergh, Garsdale and Dent* calmly suggested that Bluecaster must be the site of a barrack, yet offers no evidence. He is right to use the word 'camp' as its derivation is from *campus* meaning field. Bluecaster is certainly campestral (an open-field).

Our modern day search on the worldwideweb offers us a flood of alternatives. With water always in mind an initial glance at 'The Falls' is promising but then a second glance will confirm The Falls as a Miami shopping mall playing host to a band called Bluecaster playing live on Thursday lunch times. Sharing the bill with Atomic Cowboy and Avenging Lawn Mowers makes for an interesting trip to the shops. Not for us. A similar theme may be found with mountain and music when we consider the guitar called the Seymour Vintage Strat Bluecaster Deluxe. It is not our Bluecaster.

Closer to home the name crops up with the equine inclined. A rare steed website lists such a marvellous beast as Bluecaster Felicity (and details such as 'black markings foaled 1985') and companion classics as Lunesdale Peggy, Low Haygarth Lucy, Greenholme Tina and Hardendale Raven. There is also a Bluecaster Gracie Grundy listed in the 'mean kinship analysis' of these Fell Pony registrations. Horse lovers have always remained a breed apart to me, until now. Even though I am a lover of sheep and cattle, my equine

interest has largely remained dormant. In many people the horse is revered with a passion second to none. In researching this book, I have found myself more drawn to the horse opera as I have become closer to understanding what makes the horse lover tick. On top of this personal exploration, the history of man and the horse takes us down a different (bridle) path. Indeed, the influence of woman is somewhat significant.

Originally women rode in the same manner as men, sitting astride on cross saddles. Anne of Bohemia (1366-1394) is credited with introducing sidesaddle and another woman, Catherine de Medici (1519-1589), with turning them forward again so that they too could hunt efficiently. Marie Antoinette (1755-1793) famously rode both astride and aside. It was Elizabeth Joseph, the Empress of Austria (1837-1898) who recognised the need for the rider's body to follow the motion of the horse and no doubt was an influence on Federico Caprilli (1868-1907) who began the revolution in saddle technology. So, despite their

decorative appearance the equestrian woman is as determined and as disciplined as her horse and even with the allowance of being able to change her mind regarding the seating position she was still more creative than her male counterpart.

Of course, the male influence has to be bigger and louder and the Howgills give us a perfect example and one shrouded in mystery and, perhaps, a large element of make-believe (again, a male trait). Heading west from Bluecaster over the heart of the Howgills and nearly back to the region of White Fell Head we find ourselves on Bush Howe. Here is the Black Horse of Bush Howe, at 150 yards long and 120 yards high, the dark shale of Silurian scree takes the shape of a horse and is believed to have been shaped by man.

Such shapes are not uncommon and more common 'tourist' attractions are to be found at Uffington in Wiltshire (the White Horse) and at Uisnech in Ireland (the Mare and the Stallion). Guy Ragland Phillips in *Brigantia* purports that the Black Horse is evidence of a 'Dobbie Cult', which will have taken a spiritual and mystical hold on the local community. As a high beacon it is believed to have been used by the Morecambe Bay smugglers who could see the wet stone glinting in the sun over 20 miles away.

Phillips reports further and takes reference from the legends of Rheged (the Celtic Kingdom, not the 'themed' discovery centre near Penrith) and a horse named Du y Moroedd, translated as Black Moro, or black one of the sea. This horse was to carry men from 'Benllech of the North' along a ley line back to the coastline of Anglesey in Wales. Is Benllech our Bush Howe? What Phillips is able to observe is that the Black Horse is reminiscent of ancient French and Spanish cave paintings. Which brings the subject appropriately around to equine art.

The fascination with equine also lends itself to the art world, which we have visited in literature, paintings and sculptors of nature like Goldsworthy. The Society of Equestrian Artists promotes the practice of equestrian painting and sculpture and thereby to advance our education and appreciation of this advancing art. Bluecaster Bunter by Sue Bird is a Lost Wax Bronze climbing to seven and a half inches. Sue Bird is one of a few talented artists who can actually carry the image of the horse in art form and has built an international reputation as a painter and sculptor of the horse from close hand study. Budding equine artists may like to know that Sue uses photographs and preliminary pastels to help her capture anatomical soundness alongside individual characterisation.

Not every mention of Bluecaster on our search engine exploration is set to tantalise. One such entry makes the following description: 'The uninspiring mound ahead is called Bluecaster.' Now we know that not to be true where equine artists

and fell pony breeders are concerned but when taken in comparative scale with the rest of the fells there may be an element of truth in the statement.

Perhaps this is why the dungeonmasters I briefly mentioned when we were near Barbon have taken to it so enthusiastically being as it is what is below that counts for them. The Northern Pennine Club dive into their hobby with a keen attitude and trainspotting single-mindedness. Combining geology with hydrology, mental attention with physical athleticism, potholing must have been one of the first true extreme sports. Above the Dent fault many of the caves in this area are still not fully mapped yet it is known that the deeply stepped beds of limestone provide great risk as well as great escapism to the holer who must also be a trained diver if he is to progress.

The area provides great nomenclature too, from the obviously named Eden Sike Cave to the enticing Jingling Sike Cave. Deep Moss Pot, Black Moss Pot, Featherbed Pot and Blea Pots Lumb fall from equally romantic and colourful landmarks such as Needlehouse Gill, Whorn Gill and Clouds Gill. More relevant to our boundaries is Rawthey cave located on the Rawthey downstream of the well known and magnetically titled Lady Blue's Underwater Fantasy.

Rawthey cave is a narrow band of vertically bedded limestone that drains from Bluecaster and surrounds. Northern Pennine Club members Phil Murphy and Andrew Goddard reported a major exploration of this cave in their dive of 1996 (the first recorded exploration was in 1974 by Statham and Yeadon). Their language is as keen in exclusiveness as that of the archaeologists from our earlier tour of Crosby Fell, as Andrew explains in his description of Rawthey Cave:

On the left of the choke, a vertical slot below a large poised flake could be followed. The airbell was large with several dry leads. There was no obvious continuation to the sump. Luckily a search below water revealed a slot in the south wall and twelve inches of line was soon laid to a boulder choke. This was dug until an opening was made and the divers could pass through. After a difficult section weaving through debris

the divers soon emerged into a large tunnel. This was perfectly straight and shingle floored. After 20 metres the passage started to rise up a gravel slope and the divers surfaced in a large passage at least fifteen metres high. Two giant perpendicular flakes of rock acted like a guillotine across 90 per cent of the passage. The stream was issuing from beneath the flakes. At the top of the boulder slope there is a body-sized hole with a black void beyond.

It conjures up a better atmosphere if you sit quietly in a still chill room, close your eyes and have someone read the section to you. You may need to open your eyes sharply when you hear that Phil and Andy's recent exploits beneath Bluecaster has led to significant finds of several chambers and a very rich deposit of human and animal bones. Clearly Statham and Yeadon were not the first explorers.

Behind Bluecaster is Baugh Fell and one route away from the Howgills back into Yorkshire. We are not going that way yet, but it is worth a short diversion to visit another geological feature. The heaving monster and wilderness that is Baugh Fell was once home to a succession of mines and quarries. Kevin Lancaster reports for the Sedbergh and District History Society in his excellent short thesis appropriately titled *Mines and Quarries on Baugh Fell* that most of the action took place during the 18th and 19th centuries.

It seems that the fell was not such a quiet place and was prone to much quarry quarrelling as the business in slate and coal expanded. The raid on the fell was doomed for both products as each succumbed to competition with superior 'USPs' (unique selling points). The slate from Baugh Fell was poor in quality when compared to the hard and sharp Westmorland slate, and when the railway came to Sedbergh in 1861 coal routes from the richer deeper Durham mines were opened. The Baugh Fell mines practically disappeared overnight.

STENNERSKEUGH CLOUDS AND HARRY'S PARCEL

Looking east on the way out of the Rawthey Valley the driver and his passenger will see rolls of stone ravines in clods grouped to the horizon. It is a simple enough derivation for clods to become clouds perhaps, though still open to debate. What is clear is that Stennerskeugh Clouds has much more romance as a name than something like Stoneclough Clods.

The name playfully offers recognition and mystery in the same breath. If more than just a passing glance is possible, and time is available, then you are advised to leave the A683 just after Rawthey Bridge and to take the Uldale road that runs narrower, higher and in parallel, and thankfully, much slower than the A683 where the traffic throws itself in and out of the valley floor.

Affording the time to continue at a lesser pace, gazing eyes can wander and the car can travel at leisure, stopping to peer over the wall of a gently signposted Quaker Burial Ground between the brilliantly named Foggy Gill, Ash Pot, Elm Pot and Cold Keld habitations. The small, enclosed burial ground is very much worth the delay as a firm reminder of the Quaker heritage.

Of course what the peering person will realise when peering is that there are no gravestones in the small enclosure. Quakers believe that all ground is 'God's ground' and special consecrated ground is unnecessary, thus any convenient piece of land is acceptable for burial. There are more than 550 Quaker burial ground sites in England and Wales the majority of which use gravestones to a uniformity in respect of materials, size and even wording on the stones such that no distinction can be made between the rich and the poor. Being without any stones makes the burial ground all the more fascinating and is bound to introduce discourse about 'the meaning of death', which makes a pleasant change from the meaning of life! The Quaker view of what happens after death is principled on experience in this life and that is usually where the dogma ends.

There are some records that suggest that this higher route used to be the 'main' road when vehicles had more time, indeed, had to have more time. The views from this higher contour offer a better opportunity to appreciate the valley and recognise the demographics of the countryside. By climbing up Harter Fell, at the Sprintgill side, to look back across the Clouds and towards the fells of Wild Boar and Swarth, one can see enclosure patterns drawn like pencil lines, shaping the patchwork fields for sheep gathering, at and around our back road, before reaching the richer pasture at the bottom.

There is plenty of room to the side of the top road to leave a car, safely on the verge, for a manageable-for-all-ages walk up to and around the Clouds. As I've said before, this book is not a walking, climbing, rambling guide and how anyone approaches the Clouds is up to them. By all means, wear stilettos and a bikini, go by

Gill then Doven Gill to Sally Beck and our friend the Rawthey. Doven Gill is a Pandora's Box for the keen photographer at anytime of year: dry stream, frozen stream, stream at rush. Leaving this feature the steady observer of geological wonder should watch his step, as there is a hole of single graveyard capacity close-by. At six foot by two foot, the lonely hole looks like a ready-made tomb for the unsteady and hapless tourist.

Heading upwards, yet on a moderately gentler incline, the target should be a single tree. Now known as the Wainwright Tree because Alfred Wainwright mentions it in his Howgill book, it is a useful landmark to gain one's bearings, especially if the real clouds are blowing low. Does the tree classify as a Dowly

skateboard or paraglider, or wait until a winter night or monsoon storm.

The dictionary definition of 'in the clouds' is to lose touch with reality and to some extent this is what you can do here. Lose touch with reality. Take a dip and be hip, put a glide in the stride. Take yourself past the two very fine examples of lime kilns and skirt around the fell end to the Doven Gill, a great example of the power of water on soft limestone. Cutting beneath the shallow soil and tree roots an unusual channel has cut like the tide forcing against and beneath a boy's sand castle.

Falling down a succession of contours from Sand Tarn on Wild Boar Fell, Forcepot Sike becomes Clouds

Tree? I have also seen this written as Dawley and even Dooley, the definition is the same. A tree that grows in solitude against the odds above the treeline contradicts all manner of spatio-temporal phenomena and is known as a Dowly Tree. It shouldn't by rights be able to grow where it grows yet it does.

Running to the side of Wainwright's Tree are narrow channels that take on a man-made nature. As a low cast student of archaeological mechanics I can only offer them as miners' hushes,

as on Baugh Fell, from a time when prospecting was more common. Four caves cut into the rocks along a ledge a few hundred yards from this point suggest housing for a hermit rather than prospecting for profit. Yet the caves only dip into the stone by a few feet and would only satisfy a midget. I know that medieval stockmen used the higher ground to a greater degree than they do now and would retire to the fells for whole seasons.

Perhaps the shallow cave was a simple sanctuary against the boars and wilder beasts of the brooding moor. I would love to know what tales these shallow tunnels hold. Mesolithic hunters from eight to ten thousand years ago no doubt tracked down the beasts that roamed these fells, and in a time when they were heavily wooded, needed refuge. Perhaps they are folly founded to fool the furrowed brow of inquisitors like myself.

Across Fell End Clouds the layered limestone clints and grikes provide fun clambering and mix

low steps with high reaches, squeeze gripping fists and test tired knees. Care is needed as the protruding lump of stone that held fast for your partner may decide to be set free when it's your turn to grasp for a fix.

Harry's Parcel is the name of ruined enclosures lying immediately below the Fell End Clouds. A curious array of high square fields goes presumably by this name as a parcel of land sold to Harry. It may be presumed that this is the same Harry who lived at the smallholding in the clouds going by the name of Harry Hopes, believed to have been last inhabited in 1820. Readers wanting to know more about Henry 'Harry' Hopes should move swiftly and acquire a copy of the *Ravenstonedale Millennium Companion* (published by the Book House, Ravenstonedale, 2001).

Harry the hermit chose a solitary life on the fell and to the rest of us the bleak outlook is welcome

true stately proportions at Street.

The odd name derives from the initials of his sons Henry, William, John (sometime initialised as 'I'), Thomas and Harold. Built in 1868 by Potters of Kirkby Stephen, his house was also dismantled (in 1927) by Potters following Hewetson's death. Relics of the stonework can still be seen in the houses at the top end of Kirkby Stephen along South Road. The site is occasionally reviewed for renovation, even though it is a mammoth task with today's financial mountains, and keen entrepreneurs must remain ambitious in the hope of bringing life back to Hwith. Interestingly, in its day Hwith was taxingly pronounced to rhyme with 'tithe', yet today is more tersely pronounced to rhyme with 'pith'.

Our balloon trip around the Howgills is nearly complete and with only one watering hole left to consider, we avoid tumbling back into Kirkby Stephen and turn, by the Fat Lamb, towards Ravenstonedale.

too but we have the guarantor that we can go home to a warm fire at the end of our adventure. The ambitious walls vary in quality and rather surprisingly those that hug the closest to the steepest limestone rocks are the most intact. The 21st century shepherd still uses Harry's parcel to collect and count his flock.

Back on our lane and our journey continues most probably with a sighting of the many fell ponies roaming free on the rugged landscape. Rejoining the A685 the next signpost announces Street in the singular. By the wonderfully and imaginatively named Street amongst a wide display of trees sits the ruins of Hwith and another extraordinary tale. John Hewetson from Ellergill, half a mile to the west, headed south to seek his fortune in London. He prospered in the furniture business (the upholsterer and bedding manufacturers of Hewetson, Milner and Thexton Ltd.) and with his wealth came home to build his house of

RAVENSTONEDALE

Ravenstonedale is pleasantly situated in a hollow among the Westmorland hills, just over the Yorkshire boundary. Comparatively near are the sources of the Lune, the Eden, the Swale, the Ure, and the Rawthey. It may be reached by car from Sedbergh, through Cautley to the Rawthey bridge, beyond which turn sharply to the left and follow the ancient road, now quite passable, for about one and half miles, when the highest part of Ravenstonedale is entered; among the first of the houses stands the manse. A good road too, which passes the Kirkby Stephen railway station on the main LMS line to Scotland, leads from Kirkby Stephen over the fells to Ravenstonedale, 4.5 miles distant. Approaching the village along this route, a charming view of the Dale is obtained. The Ravenstonedale (New Biggin) railway station on the Tebay to Kirkby Stephen line is some two miles distant. Isolated, remote, unseen either from the main roads or from the railways, one can easily understand, how, in the Tudor and early Stuart Periods, this small hamlet would be a self-contained community.

Thos. Whitehead, *History of the Dales Congregational Churches*, 1932

To local people Ravenstonedale is pronounced as 'Rizundal' (or something like that). I tried to get an accurate spelling of this snappier colloquialism yet

failed and gave up after my first attempt to ask a local. When I asked how do you spell that, the answer was, of course, 'Ravenstonedale'. This dry humour was so dry I wasn't sure the character knew the joke himself.

The origin of the name, like many, is given many alternatives. One concerns an old custom in which a bounty of two pence was paid for a raven's head. An odd claim with which to name your town. I don't know how I do it but I never seem to fall into Ravenstonedale by the same route. And 'fall in' is exactly how I seem to arrive there. I always get the impression that I have arrived on a different day to the one I was in and maybe, to a parallel world of some sorts. Here there is the impression of a different society to the rest of the Howgill loop. A closed shop of sorts. Old barns have been ghost written into new halls.

Walls protecting enclosures are all complete and tall and tidy.

Wide approaches should signify its fairly recent life as a route for heavy traffic yet it is so quiet as to project the feeling that it grew from the middle and expanded exponentially with such speed that the wide road was a result. Only by coincidence did the village bounce out of its own world to touch ours and merge over an invisible barrier allowing a rippling time lapse to the corners of the village and another unseen layer within.

A simpler explanation may be to refer to Ravenstonedale as the place that is host to an eloquent and gentle Sunday evening television drama. Character actors in forgotten garb should be standing on corners waiting for their cue to provide unlikely tales to the history of the village. It needs no make-believe history, no sub-soap script and certain no Hollywood treatment. The proprietors of Ravenstonedale have scribed their own eloquence in annals of literature. From the Rev. W. Nicholls and Thos Whitehead over a century

ago to the townsfolk's own Millennium recordings facilitated by the town's own publishers at The Book House, the chronology of Ravenstonedale is delivered on a plate yet still retains an air of complete mystery and detachment. The whole town is an odd corner.

The street map appears to me to be upside down, or inside out, thus qualifying the alternate universe. The list of old buildings seems greater than the actual number of buildings visible. The protection offered by high walls fail to declare if they are keeping people out or keeping people in. I am never clear whether it is a sanctuary or a sanatorium!

Ravenstonedale attracts whom it attracts and throughout history it has achieved a unique identity and reflected elitism. Its command of the relationship between religion and power is second to none throughout the Howgills and indeed throughout Cumbria. It has proved to be a magnet to prayer and discipline for a thousand years and perhaps that same monastic order and principles of separation afford this unique balance of frictioned unity.

Many roots lie with the Gilbertines and the decayed foundations of the Gilbertine Priory ruins beside St. Oswald's church, which we shall come to later. Gilbert (born in 1085) was the son of a Norman knight with William the Conqueror, and a mother of Saxon origin. It was his mother who was said to have dreamed before Gilbert's birth that she was holding the round moon (Lune?) in her lap, which was taken to be a sign that the child would rise to greatness.

Gilbert turned to the priesthood after a difficult upbringing caused by a deformity and social exclusion. He founded a convent at Sempringham in Lincolnshire with the express aim that women could retire from the world in order to devote themselves to study and worship. Sempringham Priory was founded in 1135 and the Pope, the King and Bishop Alexander of Lincoln approved the new Order of Gilbertines.

Gilbertine Priories were founded at Alvingham, North Ormsby, Six Hills, West Torrington and Lincoln. Others followed until there was a total of thirteen houses for women. Eventually, and inevitably men were introduced into the houses to help with the heavy duties but were kept in disciplined separation from the nuns. I applaud Gilbert's values, as he had a great interest in education and lived by example not only by his own learning but also by his humility and energy.

After Gilbert's death in 1189 (aged 104), the Order continued to grow and at the Dissolution there were 26 Gilbertine houses in England. This has been the only Monastic Order ever to originate in England (the others coming from Europe) and as such the remains of the Gilbertine Priory beside St. Oswald's are very precious and by default they are odd. St. Oswald, who now sits in Gilbert's place, is no less odd.

The Church of St Oswald (Church of England) was completed in 1744 and before taking a short tour we should consider the merits of St. Oswald too. Born in 605, the son of the pagan King Aethelfrith the Ravager of Bernicia and Princess Aacha of Deira, Oswald was the second of seven children and brother of Saint Ebbe the Elder. Significantly for us, Oswald is said to have had a pet raven and a raven is seen on his shoulder in many of the drawings and stained glass window characterisations of him.

It is said that at Oswald's wedding to the daughter of King Cynegils of Wessex, a raven brought him the wedding ring. In 634, Oswald formed his own army, returned to Northumbria, defeated King Cadwallon of Gwynedd, and took the throne of Northumbria. Prior to the battle, he had received a vision of Saint Colman; he had also erected a large cross on the field on the night before, attributed his win to his faith and the intervention of the saint, and the victory is famously known as the Battle of Heavenfield.

Even though he was clearly a warrior of some ilk, Oswald built monasteries and brought in monks from Scotland to help establish monastic life, most notably St. Aiden at Lindisfarne. We find St. Aiden again as the dedicated host to a building, now of secular use, in Newbiggin-on-Lune. St. Oswald himself is remembered in other locales such as Grasmere and Horton-in-Ribblesdale, and, of course, Kirkoswald, which has the river Raven Beck. There are some writings that explore Oswald's actions and faith with an alternate eastern character with the title Isapostolos.

Oswald was killed in battle against invading pagan Mercian and Welsh armies on 5 August 642 at Maserfield, Shropshire. As such he is often listed as a martyr. It is reported that he died praying for the souls of his bodyguards

and compatriots. There was clearly anger in the battle as Oswald's body was hacked to pieces with his head and arms stuck on poles. Dismembered limbs eventually found there way to relic collections in monasteries around England; his remaining body was buried first at Bardney Abbey, Lincolnshire, and later moved to Saint Oswald's church, Gloucester.

Significantly for us, the collectors of visceral ephemera also included his pet raven who, the story says took one arm to an ash tree. Where the arm fell to the ground, a holy well sprang up. The holy water spring may not be related to that barely a mile away as the River Lune springs at St. Helen's Well, but there can be no doubt about the connection of the raven. Martyrdom offers a link too as the church of St. Oswald proudly displays a stained-glass window commemorating the death of Elizabeth Gaunt who we met earlier in the book at Newbiggin. The beautiful church is also unique for its inward-facing pews and unusual three-decker pulpit.

The tower to the church was built a few years before the church and used to stand alone. It provides a good example of the odd rules of the village. The tower stood on pillars with openings on each side to the bell rope hanging in the centre. This was an adult version of 'home' or 'home-base' used by children in playgrounds throughout the land as a place of safety and sanctuary. Their games may be simple 'tig' or 'tag', but the Ravenstonedale Refuge Bell gave anyone ringing

it safety over any chasing sheriff, or any other officer of the King. There was a flaw however as ringing the bell may have meant security from the national laws and regulations but it also meant that the offender must be tried by the rules of Ravenstonedale, and leniency was not a natural progression.

Ravenstonedale had its own court, with 24 jurors presiding. Anyone seeking trial outside the parish was fined so in reality the ringing of the bell did little to protect the guilty. Eavesdropping was a chargeable offence, which maybe explains the lack of coffee shops and teahouses in Ravenstonedale. Houses were not to be let to foreigners, or visitors from outside the dale. I imagine the arrival of out comers who can comfortably commute to Manchester and Glasgow from the village has altered the economies of this law.

Football was forbidden; clearly a relic left over from the female dominated Gilbertine ideals.

neighbour to the softer named High and Low Chapels.

The High Chapel claims to be the oldest non-conformist chapel in the country and it is fitting that, after a tour of the Howgills that has visited so much reform (of religious and scientific worth), that we finish our journey at such a site. How appropriate too that the chapel now plays host to the congregation of the United Reformed Church. Whilst their brief for Christian worship may not be pluralist, the term of United Reform certainly sits fairly amongst Howgill principles.

Indeed, the female folk were in a state of power as a 'majority of females' instated a law that forbade bachelors to marry outside the parish unless he paid a penalty of £20 and suffered imprisonment for ten months after marriage. I would like to add a cynical comment about fines, marriage and imprisonment but this is probably not the place.

The Peculiar Court of Ravenstonedale mirrors what many consider to be peculiar people. It may be true that peculiar people wear peculiar spectacles, but this is a valid example of the diversity of peoples combined with a common cause. There has been enough freedom in the village to allow independent voice and the existence of Primitive Methodist Chapel (1873), Wesleyan Chapel (1839), and Independent Chapel (1727) and out at Fell End, the Ravenstonedale Friends Meeting House (1705) as denominational faiths rise and fall in favour. Today the religious fervour is mannered in quieter fashion as St. Oswald's plays

As we leave behind the high walls, built to protect the ancient deer park of Lord Wharton, and giant's graves, believed to be rabbit mounds farmed by the monks for the simple pleasure and necessity of food, where next do we wander off? For the time being our searching is done. Time to reflect, time to consider the changes that have been made and the changes we still need to make.

WATERSHED

The way the river flows from the fell decides many things as it leaves barren land to one side and lush pasture suitable for settlement to the other. The watershed of the many rivers around the Howgills and North Pennines has contrived to provide the destiny for everyone in the area. Here the Lune and the Eden take on parental roles and what icons to our very being they are. Yet, it has not always been that way. These rivers too took different forms and geologists from far and wide come to our region as once more the Howgills illustrate their uniqueness.

We know that the Eden is rare in flowing north, yet not many realise that there is good evidence to suggest that the Lune also took a similar path. This is not the place to embroil the readership with geological terms such as Mesozoic, Eocene and Anticline so we shall accept the theories without further detail. It appears that the Lune Spring once headed in the direction of Potts Beck and Scandal Beck; and further downstream the Carling Gill took a northerly route towards and past Tebay.

Celebrated geologist Professor Marr described the river captures of the Howgills and Northern Pennines as illustrating the 'law of unequal slopes.' So, even the watershed, the dividing line, the decision maker, can change and need to change from time to time.

This brings in another dimension, one of

time, something we have little control over. In our daily living, our lifetime we must recognise the watershed and make sure the next steps for change are firm. Geological time is beyond our ken. We are but insignificant beings in comparison to the perpetual waters of the Lune and her fabulous fells and in many ways it is reassuring to have the same earth beneath our feet as our ancestors and our ancestors' ancestors.

We can observe a spiritual psychology of the geographical watershed and the symbolisation of water taking a decision to turn one way down the fell. Like life, we are faced with watersheds, through circumstance and through choice. Or we could just let go and see what happens.

Watershed: what a lovely word that is, and what a picture it brings to mind! Perhaps only those who have fallen under the spell of the tops and the watersheds can really understand what it means... Once you fall under the spell of the watersheds and the high and lonely places, you will not be happy away from them for long. It is a curious choice, perhaps, this desire to climb to the roof of the world... Heath and bracken all the way there, and peat hags, whams and bogs when you get there... For me at any rate, there is a particular exultation in making my way, preferably alone or with one kindred spirit only... Nothing has changed here for aeons, or so it seems; nothing disturbs the serenity of the mind as one wanders alone over the wild wastelands. This is the world as it was in the beginning of time, is now, and ever shall be; and you are alone with Nature - or with God.

Alfred J Brown, *Broad Acres*, 1949

BIG CORNERS, LITTLE COACHES - MOTORWAYS AND BUSES

During the latter part of my pharmaceutical years in the south of England I, like many, was faced with the prospect of redundancy. Brainstorming career options with my business colleague, Vince, we came up with the idea of taking a six-month tour of every motorway junction in the land and writing a guidebook of hostelries and fuel stops. The marketability was obvious, as we did not know of anyone who enjoyed the abject horror of the typical British Motorway Service Station.

Six months or so after our very fine idea the very same book was in print only we were not the authors. I am glad enough to recommend this book to other motorway users and I am sad enough to own quite a few guidebooks to our motorways. *Off the Motorway* by Paul and Shirley Smith (2000) lists places of interest within in a reasonable distance from every motorway junction in the country.

Whilst I recommend the book it gives a paltry account of our stretch from Junction 36 to 39. Kirkby Lonsdale, Sedbergh, Kendal and Kirkby Stephen are given as 'sites of interest' and that's it! Indeed, it leaves Junction 39 blank and the driver must assume no sites of interest. The Smiths may have been sharper than me and Vince but the job had actually been done before.

Off the Motorway by Christopher Pick (1984) focused in a little more detail regarding the options for the tourist wanting to explore more than just a need for a half hour tea and toilet stop.

At Junction 36 he recommends Levens Hall and Sizergh Castle, at 37 he directs us to picnic sites at Killington Reservoir (hurrah!) but then lets himself down by adding that 'Now the motorway runs deep through the Cumberland Fells... on the borders of the Lakes and Yorkshire Dales' and then throws his hat in the ring with the incredible statement 'Junction 38 is in lower, rather uninteresting country with nothing special to leave the motorway for.' We now know different.

Junction 38 is but three miles from Orton Scar, three miles from Howgill village, three miles from Bretherdale and has to be, without contradiction, the best motorway junction in the world. I suppose the dismal adverts from both these books are what help to keep the motorist passing through. We need some, for essential trade, but if we right the balance of change then I actually thank Messrs Smith and Pick for their poor coverage. Pick does alert us to Shap Abbey and Lowther Castle when he reaches Junction 39 and in every other respect it is a fine volume.

In my opinion the best offering for our stretch comes in the dedicated booklet *The M6 from*

Forton to Penrith, a Dalesman mini-book (1971). It's date and size make it difficult to track down although I am sure one of the many stall holders of Sedbergh Book Town will have a copy. Author E. Peter Johnson gives routes left, right and sideways from each of the junctions and carefully lists the road numbers and sights both northbound and southbound. For example, at Junction 38 Southbound he describes observations to be found from the B470, B469, B468, B467, B466, B465, B464, B463 and B462. It borders on dreaded statistics yet is really well put together.

Ironically one of the most significant motorway books is *Around the M25* by John Burke (1986). I can forgive the M25 book for not mentioning the route across the area covered by this book yet the circular route of over 100 miles serves to give gratitude for what we have with our zip-fastener M6. I don't think I need explain at length except to ask you to imagine the M25 picked up and dropped on our route from Kirkby Stephen, Orton, Tebay, Grayrigg, Killington, Kirkby Lonsdale, Middleton, Sedbergh, Cautley and Ravenstonedale. It might not be 100 miles yet it is so much more.

I am sure everyone has his or her favourite motorway. The M6 is the spine of England with organs beating throughout its curvature - Birmingham and Spaghetti Junction, to the Manchester and Liverpool networks, and then the falling mirage of the Borders. I am not fond of all of it, yet our stretch in the Howgills continues to send goosebumps down my spine. Special to me because it signifies home and arrival home at that - after a long arduous patient journey past the mountains of miserable Midlands, past the moors of muddled Merseyside and Mancunia, and before the pale passport to Scotland.

An obvious scar on the landscape, it is actually good for the preservation of the peace and pace

that the motorway and railway are here in the Howgills. They speed people through and contamination is left to a minimum and any such influence is made by comparable souls who have made the choice to stop

A swift reminder of the route begins with the shingled hill of Farleton Knott above Kirkby Lonsdale and Junction 36 below. To the left above Crooklands we see the shining beacon at St. Patrick's and our first key for home. Signposts call for the South Lakes and the new visitor centre will add a further beacon for the blind tourist. Indeed, in the last year the proposed new visitor centre, planned to enhance the gateway to the lakes has diminished from our newspapers being replaced by talk of a new business park. Hardly the eye candy needed to welcome guests.

It is not too long ago that traffic used to disappear at Preston and the route north was one of peace and space. Not any more, the road is as busy up to Junction 36 and is getting heavier every day. This is not a good prospect. The Howgills and the Yorkshire Dales are not mentioned on these signposts. Thank you for that.

Junction 37 is remote, simple as that. Perfect in some timeless virginity. Few come off here. Eyes wander west to the tall framed windmills and then sharply back to the road as the descent into the Lune Gorge. Jaw dropping. The motorway runs parallel to the railway, which even in electrification adds to the mixed boundaries of time, then dissects the Howgills as they rise up around in all directions, and dimensions. The *tromp l'oiel* imagery can be intoxicating as heads turn and arms reach out in some vague expectancy of being able to touch the distant peaks.

I have alluded to Junction 38 already yet it is worthy of mention again simply for the slip road which merits odd corner status. A 50 mile-an-hour speed limit is most valid as are four wheels firmly on the ground, as the looping exit seems to go on forever. At the Tebay roundabout we see the great signs of new tourism. The brown backgrounded sign displays an annoyingly frequency from time to time and whilst a fan of the aesthetic in signposts generally, we now have far too many of them.

Junction 39 must be the smallest and bleakest of all England's motorway junctions. If joining the motorway, the slip roads give you two options: Lancaster the South and Carlisle the North. Not a great choice. But then you have most likely just come from Shap. The name derives from *hep* or *heppe* which itself relates to heps of hips, another name for the fruit of the rose-hip. The slang term for Shap is anciently known as Choop, the dialect word for the rose-hip. Indeed, hip Shap is upwardly ship-shape. Shap is re-inventing itself.

Stories of tragic weather and hardship are buffeted by achievement and heroic action both before the motorway and during its relatively short term. It may have replaced the A6 over Shap Fell as the West Coast artery: it suffers the same lack of elemental control. The Shap road was, and still is, notorious for becoming blocked by snow at all times of year.

The first stage coach over Shap was in 1763 and modernisation took some time before the current Shap road opened in 1823 to replace the old Kendal turnpike. It was always in the national news headlines, along with its three friends the Lakeland Kirkstone Pass, the Alston road over the Pennines and the A66 across Stainmore.

The Highways Agency has come up with a M6 route management strategy and a plan for the next ten years for the route from Warrington to Scotland, focusing on accident clusters, regular congestion spots, poor lane discipline, and slip-road access. The problems between Junction 36 and 39 are more specific and concern an unwanted frequency of night time accidents, major bridge

repairs and continuing problems with wind (rather than the snow of old).

Shap rarely gets mentioned now, as the motorway is hyperlinked to the media and radio-monitored virtual flying eyes. As I said before, if the M6 keeps on moving then perhaps 'they' will work quietly too and leave us alone. At least one turn of modernisation and regulatory requirement has made me smile.

In some sort of Andy Goldsworthy pillory, power firm United Utilities have surrounded a mobile phone transmitter antenna at Junction 39 of the M6 with a stone wall *a la* Goldsworthy Sheepfold. It probably serves, by imitation, to promote the Goldsworthy show and whether it is classified as art with a function, or a function with a bit of art is open to conjecture. What is clear is that the technology of linking the antenna to the adjacent National Grid pylon is one of the first of its kind in the country, again showing our region to be on board for reform, this time in the new age of communication technologies. I doubt, however, if the powers that be are planning to 'sheepfold' the landmarking electricity pylons.

At the foot of the western slopes of the hills, Howgill is worth seeking out along twisting roads between high banks. A narrow lane only suited to local traffic, either ends so far as the motorist is concerned, or branches to cross Crook of Lune Bridge into Westmorland; and through this sequestered vale is to run a great

modern trunk-road, which is planned to pass up the west side of England... On the other side of the Howgills, Cautley might be just as remote valley as this, but instead a main road busy with traffic, the turnpike from Sedbergh to Kirkby Stephen on route from Blackpool to Newcastle, passes through it. Few trunk-roads in England have a finer setting than this at Cautley

Marie Hartley and Joan Ingilby, *The Yorkshire Dales*, 1956

With the titular subject of Odd Corners I cannot ignore the very things that use the corners. In the main this is me, and you, and friends of all dates, duties and descriptions. It is also our carriages into those corners, and out again, and this may be any vessel from a pair of well-worn boots to a luxurious steam train of old.

The train is an icon of transport and clearly drives a large percentage of keen pencil case holders and the literary produce from fans of the iron giants is ubiquitous. The common or garden bus and her rural route renders less attention. In my small way, I will attempt some form of redress.

Potts Valley has already been home to my tale of the school minibus. As teenagers we were also taken with the hospitality of the coach taking us on rugby tours and in particular, the local bus service that was Ribble. Ridicule was the nature of the day, we were Ribble rousers, and while the Ribble duly performed to the highest degree expected, mockery became the best form of compliment. Speed, well lack of it, timeliness, well lack of it, and comfort, enough said.

The drivers were the stars. Known affectionately with any name that sat between the Good, the Bad and the Ugly and with temperaments to match, the fun of the ride was governed by the driver of the day. Whoever drove with the Ribble bus service, most of the journey was spent an inch above the seat as bottoms bounced a split second behind the timing of the bus as it lurched into the wide swing of a corner or took a see-saw effect when encountering a humpback bridge.

The cold windows were always steamed up allowing the childlike artist to write mirrored words for those outside. On cold days the under seat heater would be off. On warm days it would be blasting out hot air. Every seat had an ashtray. Every ashtray was full. The clock at the front was only correct twice a day. Circular scars of removed chewing gum on the tatty upholstery

served only as a frustrating reminder to the one in the gang who had stamped his plimsoll hard on the discarded gum on the floor.

The best place to sit was a constant debate, but only in your own head as peer pressure took control. It had to be at the back although who of the ten clambered in the seven spaces meant for five would rest with the order of the wolf pack. In the back row observation was key. All peers and servants turning to bow with heads on high headrests. All threats of seniority in the front and their sways and lunges synchronised with the route of the bus. And the most dangerous threat to power, the driver, being locked in his duty and too far to be heard with his cries of 'sit down' 'shut up' and 'I know who you are.'

Of course, we had it wrong. The best place was right at the front, on the shoulder of the driver. A place not only to note the route but also to collect the wisdom of the man behind the wheel. This wisdom may be misplaced from time to time and a disciplined editorial ear would serve well. The

covert spying nature of the Chinese whisperers suited those inclined towards tea rooms and ready to rush to ruminating rumours. Sat in rows four and five gave these ears enough material to formulate their own devices for high drama over coffee and scone. Indeed, the *Dalesman* magazine recognised the anecdotal source, as a humourous complement to Old Amos and Young Fred, in a regular feature called *Heard in a Dales Bus*.

It is clear that the bus is a very different entity to the train. Trainspotters do not sit and chat with the train driver. As a general rule, passengers on trains do not lend themselves to the local gossip and conjecture that is heard on the bus. The bus is more intimate. Trainspotters stand at the end of Platform 4 and scribble notes in their little black books. Railway photographers seek out deserted stations and stand with camera bags, tripods and SLR at the ready.

I have never seen a bus-spotter standing at a bus stop with his notebook in his hand and compact poised. Indeed, I don't think I have ever seen a bus-spotter. Bus spotting is clearly more discrete. Rest assured, it goes on. Please can you stand up if you are a bus spotter? Ahem, no standing on the bus, thank you. The bus enthusiast does subscribe to middle shelf magazines in a similar fashion to the railway fan and if you stand in your newsagent you will see him there searching for *Bus and Coach Enthusiast* or *Tram and Trolleybus* or *Bus Collector*.

There is another similarity between the busophile and the trainophile however and this falls into the lap of our old friend the statistician. The deregulation of the bus services in the UK through the Deregulation Act of 1986 has given many people the opportunity to carry clip boards, calculate customers and costs and carry on at some length about the demise of local services. Taking variables such as wait time, walk time and journey time in contrast with vehicle and service quality our stimulated statistician can tell us the Consumer Surplus (CS - the benefit obtained by bus users over and above the fare they pay) and prove that they think they are more intelligent than us by offering us:

$$CS = \int_{P}^{\infty} Q \, dP = 1/b \, (0 - Q) = (-1/b) \, Q$$

Very good, go to the top of the class. Bus deregulation meant no public transport for many communities and a transition into decay with the closure of rural schools, rural amenities such as health services confirms our government's preoccupation with the economies of density. The pendulum swings again and some bus routes are being re-invented to serve the community well.

However, understanding the bus route and its times is a trick only known to experienced locals and frequent users. Heaven help the tourist who stands at the stop by Sedbergh Market Square at 9.45 on a Friday wanting to go to Kirkby Lonsdale without realising it only travels on a Thursday. Or the same fellow on a Wednesday who standing outside the Dalesman in Sedbergh for the 10.00 to Hawes doesn't know it only goes on a Tuesday. Such problems are sent as challenges only and the advanced bus traveller can actually makes great use of our little network. Where else would you consider an hour's tour from Sandford (near Warcop) to Kirkby Stephen, Ravenstonedale, Newbiggin and Brough finishing at Crosby Garrett? It's a Grand Prix circuit.

There are no super buses or 'posh' coaches with tables and toilets. There are no urban double-deckers with 'plenty of room on top.' There are quite a few varieties of little bus however, each with their own style and personality and favourite driver. I would recommend everyone try a bus ride, while they can. It's cheap (it is, especially compared to running your own car), you get a better view and after all, what is the point of rushing. If we all slow down we will all live a little longer.

One of the nicest ways is to make use of the Cumbria Classic Coaches out of Bowber Head at Ravenstonedale. Of course, our route around the Howgills fulfils its circle as it is these machines that we see head off from the Commercial Vehicle Rally we met at Kirkby Stephen in the first chapter. Old coaches made new that may bounce along the roads yet they do it at a civilised pace conducive with our Howgills. My favourite is their 33 seater AEC Regal from 1948, called Florence. Increasingly popular for days out and special occasions the Classic Coaches provide the perfect medium for nostalgia and reflection. It is a marvellous way to get familiar with the Howgills; whether viewing detailed panoramas or odd corners, whether viewing the changing seasons so dramatic in the spring and autumn, or whether simply reflecting on what has been and what will be.

Paradigm

I was going to call this work 'Naked in the Howgills' to emphasise the personal tales and feelings for the fells and the intimacy of spirit I am able to share. Even though it mirrored Wordsworth's *Naked Heights of the Howgills*, my alternative title conjured up too many alternatives in subject matter and while I may enjoy Howgill nakedness I do not want to offend. Yet it would have suited the Howgill's naturalness of reflective peace and pace.

The pleasures that we cannot remember are the most rewarding and most desired, especially the simplest - taste, sex, freedom and unencumbered playfulness. More emotional triggers, from child-like naivety to the achievement of challenge and granted solitude by being on top of a fell, are stimulated on top of the Howgills and around the Howgills. It is a place where inner discovery is most important and with that there is still room to breathe.

The term global village is accurate in terms of describing the scale of our increasingly diminishing planet, yet the scale of meaning in the words are being lost. The Lake District and Cumbria has leisure parks that by their nature disembowel their original meaning. Leisure? Park? Themed amusement villages rip apart any personal imagination. Orange replaces green. We are forced to believe that it is sunny every day. We could be anywhere.

Make no mistake, the Lake District is astonishing, the North Pennines are awesome, and the Yorkshire Dales outstanding. My point goes nationwide and surely this drive towards escapism and virtual reality simply takes people further away from real reality and in doing so breeds frustration, resentment, and anger as satisfaction is never achieved.

And all this while the real world is actually there on our doorstep. The Howgills are real. For today. My ethics are about attraction, not promotion. I hope to have been able to shed some light on the history of the Howgills and its people and by doing so offer some projection of experience, faith and hope for its secure future.

In the words of Will Hayes, 'education is light' and if my short educational discourse inspires readers to visit and revisit then our experience becomes shared. And in terms of world knowledge and in our little odd corner of the global village the connections we make are the most important. Curiously, you may find it interesting to know that 'I know' in Hebrew is interpreted as 'I have heard'; in Greek it is closer in meaning to 'I have seen'; and to the silent fellowship of the Quakers, born around the Howgills, it means 'I have experienced and I am still experiencing'.

Such matrices of concept kindly bring forward our understanding of the church, and by no small connection in the Howgills, the chapel. The history of a chapel takes on a deeper form. It is the history of the souls it has saved, the men it has formed, the lives it has inspired and the good it has witnessed.

I am not sure if you can plan dreams, yet I am sure you can prepare for them. As personality changes over time and is influenced by a growing maturity, key life events serve to trigger a new birth, a watershed, in some cases another chance. In its unfaltering timeless beauty I occasionally think of the Howgills as home, my spiritual home, whereas Appleby, my place of birth, is simply my physical home.

Spurred by the works of my Great Uncle Will and our shared belief that you can only achieve true intra-faith by understanding inter-faith, the Howgills give me some sort of contentment in knowing that I may yet still have to

dream that perfect dream. Will Hayes worked alongside one of the most respected Unitarians in Margaret Barr. It was the universal soul Margaret Barr who, somewhat controversially, preferred to use the word fellowship instead of church when describing the followers of faith and common belief.

Not only did she want to avoid previous perceptions, whatever their form, of the word church, she felt that fellowship more accurately described the community and the spirit within. I like to think of the people of Howgill as a fellowship. I agree with Troeltsch, we get our ethics from our history and judge our history by our ethics. Margaret Barr's works are equally compelling and with regard to this work provide astounding relevance:

Someone once asked Gandhi if he had mystical experiences and he replied, 'If by mystical experiences you mean visions and trances and that sort of thing, no. I should be a fraud if I claimed anything like that. But I am very sure of the voice that guides me.' That is exactly how I feel. Mystical experiences such as Emily Bronte describes in some of her more striking poems I know nothing of. But as I mentioned in the first chapter, the splendid assurance of her 'Last Lines' that the God within her breast was none other than the Spirit which wide-embracing love animates eternal years, pervades and broods above - this is the heart and soul of my faith too, the faith that arms against fear.

Margaret Barr, *A Dream Come True*, 1974

LAST LINES

No coward soul is mine,
No trembler in the world`s storm - troubled sphere:
I see Heaven's glories shine,
And faith shines equal, arming me from fear.
O God within my breast,
Almighty, ever - present Deity!
Life - that in me has rest,
As I - undying Life - have power in Thee!
Vain are the thousand creeds
That move men's hearts: unutterably vain;
Worthless as wither'd weeds,
Or idlest froth amid the boundless main,
To waken doubt in one
Holding so fast by Thine infinity;
So surely anchor'd on
The steadfast rock of immortality.
With wide - embracing love
Thy Spirit animates eternal years,
Pervades and broods above,
Changes, sustains, dissolves, creates, and rears.
Though earth and man were gone,
And suns and universes cease to be,
And Thou were left alone,
Every existence would exist in Thee.
There is not room for Death,
Nor atom that his might could render void:
Thou - Thou art Being and Breath,
And what Thou art may never be destroyed

Emily Bronte, 1844

BIBLIOGRAPHY, SOURCES AND RECOMMENDED READING

Afoot in the Yorkshire Dales, HO Wade, 1981

Andy Goldsworthy Sheepfolds, Michael Hue-Williams, 1996

Arch, Andy Goldsworthy & David Craig, 1999

Birds of the Yorkshire Dales, WR Mitchell, 1998

Bridges of Lancashire and Yorkshire, Margaret Slack, 1986

British Bus Systems number two, Ribble, Eric Ogden, 1983

British Railways Past and Present No. 1 Cumbria, J Houghton & N Harris, 1985

Book of the Cow, A Study in Comparative Religion, Will Hayes, 1930

Chapels in the Valley, D Ben Rees, 1975

Church Planting, A Study of Westmorland Nonconformity, Alan PF Sell, 1986

Coast to Coast Walk, A Wainwright, 1973

Countrygoer's North, Jessica Lofthouse, 1965

County Churches, Cumberland and Westmorland, J Charles Cox, 1913

Cumbrian Yew Book, Ken Mills, 1999

Dales Way, the, Terry Marsh, 1992

Early Friends in Dent, David Boulton, 1986

Flora of Westmorland, Albert Wilson, 1938

Forbidden Land, the Struggle for Access to Mountain and Moorland, Tom Stephenson, 1989

Foot and Mouth, Heart and Soul, Caz Graham, 2001

From Source to Sea, Peter R Williamson, 2001

Frontier, Forts and Farms, Cumbrian Aerial Survey, Higham & Jones, Archaeological Journal, 1975

George Fox and the Valiant Sixty, Elfrida Vipont, 1975

Gods and Myths of Northern Europe, Davidson, H. R. Ellis, 1968,

Gray Ridge, the Book of Francis Howgill, Will Hayes, 1942

Green Tracks on The Pennines, Arthur Raistrick, 1962

High Dale Country, WR Mitchell, 1991

Historical Kirkby Stephen and North Westmorland, RR Sowerby, 1950

Historic County Churches of the Lune, John L Hamer, 1960s

Historic Farmhouses in and around Westmorland, JH Palmer, 1945

History of Dales Congregational Churches, Thos Whitehead, 1932

History of Westmorland, Richard S Ferguson, 1894

Howgill Fells and their Topography, the, Geological Society, J Marr, 1909

Howgill and Dentdale, A David Leather, 1993

In Search of Westmorland, Charlie Emett, 1985

Introducing Quakers, George H Gorman, 1969

Lancashire Westmorland Highway, Jessica Lofthouse, 1953

Legends of Westmorland and other poems, Anthony Whitehead, 1952 (first pub. 1856)

Let Your Lives Speak, Elfrida Vipont Foulds, 1953

Lune Sketchbook, a, A Wainwright, 1980

M6 from Forton to Penrith, the, E Peter Johnson, 1971

Man, Society and Religion, Essay in Bridge-Building (Swarthmore Lecture), W Russell Brain, 1944

Memories of Orton, A Westmorland Parish Remembered, various, 1998

New Silurian Graptolites from the Howgill Fells, Palaeontology, R Rickards, 1965

Odd Corners in English Lakeland, WT Palmer, 1936

Odd Corners in the Yorkshire Dales, WT Palmer, 1937

Off the Motorway, Christopher Pick, 1984

Off the Motorway, Paul & Shirley Smith, 2000

Old Parish Churches of Cumbria, Mike Salter, 1998

Outstanding Churches in the Yorkshire Dales, Val Leigh, 1983

Over Shap to Carlisle, Harold D Bowtell, 1983

Picturesque Tourism, Ian Whyte, Regional Bulletin 14, Lancaster University, 2000

Portrait in Grey, John Punshon, 1984

Portrait of the Howgills and the Upper Eden Valley, Michael Ffinch, 1982

Quaker Meeting Houses, David M Butler, 1995

Quaker Meeting Houses of the Lake Counties, David M Butler, 1978

Quakers in North-west England 1, The Man in Leather Breeches, Donald A Rooksby, 1994

Quakers in North-west England 2, A People to be Gathered, Donald A Rooksby, 1995

Quakers in North-west England 3, And Sometime Upon the Hills, Donald A Rooksby, 1998

Railways of Cumbria, Peter W Robinson, 1980

Ravenstonedale with Newbiggin-on-Lune Parish Millennium Map (and Companion), various, 2001

Relic Surfaces of the Howgill Fells, Geological Society, R McConnell, 1939

Return to the Lune Valley, Stan & Freda Trott, 1972

Rufus Jones, Master Quaker, David Hinshaw, 1951

Secrets and Legends of Old Westmorland, Dawn Robertson & Peter Koronka, 1992

Sedbergh, Garsdale and Dent, W Thompson, 1892

Stainmore & Eden Valley Railways, Peter Walton, 1992

Sweet Calamus, Will Hayes, 1931

These We Have Known, Stories of Sedbergh People, Freda Trott, 2002

Verge of Lakeland, WT Palmer, 1938

Walking Down the Lune, Robert Swain, 1992

Walking in the Yorkshire Dales, Colin Speakman, 1982

Walking Roman Roads In Lonsdale and the Eden Valley, Philip Graystone, 2002,

Walking the Howgills, Mary Welsh, 1998

Walks In North Westmorland, Sir Clement Jones, 1955

Watermills of Cumbria, Mike Davies-Shiel, 1978

Wild Flowers & Where To Find Them in Northern England, Laurie Fallows, 2004

Westmorland Heritage Walk, Mark Richards & Christopher Wright, 1987

West Riding of Yorkshire, Arthur Raistrick, 1970

Wharfedale to Westmorland, Historic Walks through the Yorkshire Dales, Aline Watson, 1994

Yorkshire Dales, the, Marie Hartley & Joan Ingilby, 1956

And many pieces and features from The Dalesman, Cumbria Magazine and, of course, the Transactions of the Cumberland & Westmorland Antiquarian & Archaeological Society.

MORE BOOKS FROM HAYLOFT

Odd Corners in Appleby, Gareth Hayes (£8.50, ISBN 1 9045240 0 1)

Running High, The First Continuous Traverse of the 303 Mountains of Britain and Ireland, Hugh Symonds, (£16.99, ISBN 190 452 415X)

Behind Chained Gates, Moira Linaker (£10, ISBN 190 452 4168)

Not S'many Cows and a Lot Less Yows, Mike Sanderson (£9.95, ISBN 190 452 4087)

Yows & Cows, A Bit of Westmorland Wit, Mike Sanderson (£7.95, ISBN 0 9523282 0 8)

To Bid Them Farewell, A Foot & Mouth Diary, Adam Day (£14.50, ISBN 190 452 4109)

The Herdwick Country Cook Book, Hugh & Therese Southgate (Hardback, £29.95, ISBN 0954071182/ Paperback, £14.95, ISBN 0954071174)

Those Were the Days, An Entertainment Revue of Carlisle, 1950-70, Marie Dickens & Geoff Dickens (£22.90, ISBN 190 452 4125)

Oil, Sand & Politics, Dr. Philip Horniblow (£25, ISBN 190 452 4095)

From the High Pennines, A History of the Aldersons, Marmaduke Alderson, (£10.00, ISBN 190 452 4079)

The Maddison Line, A Journalist's Journey around Britain, Roy Maddison (£10.00, ISBN 1 9045240 6 0)

Pashler's Lane, A Clare Childhood, Elizabeth Holdgate (£10.00, ISBN 095 4207203)

The Long Day Done, Jeremy Rowan-Robinson (£9.50, ISBN 1 9045240 4 4)

The Ghastlies, Trix Jones and Shane Surgey (£3.99, ISBN 1 9045240 4 4)

A Journey of Soles, Lands End to John O'Groats, Kathy Trimmer (£9.50, 1 9045240 5 2)

Changing the Face of Carlisle, The Life and Times of Percy Dalton, City Engineer and Surveyor, 1926-1949, Marie K. Dickens (£8, ISBN 0 9540711 9 0)

From Clogs and Wellies to Shiny Shoes, A Windermere Lad's Memories of South Lakeland, Miles R. M. Bolton (£12.50, ISBN 1 9045240 2 8)

A History of Kaber, Helen McDonald and Christine Dowson, (£8, ISBN 0 9540711 6 6)

A Dream Come True, the Life and Times of a Lake District National Park Ranger, David Birkett (£5.50, ISBN 0 9540711 5 8)

Gone to Blazes, Life as a Cumbrian Fireman, David Stubbings (£9.95, ISBN 0 9540711 4 X)

Changing Times, A History of Bolton, Barbara Cotton (£12.50, ISBN 0 9540711 3 1)

Better by Far a Cumberland Hussar, A History of the Westmorland and Cumberland Yeomanry, Colin Bardgett (Hardback, £26.95, ISBN 0954071123/ Paperback, £16.95, ISBN 0954071115)

Northern Warrior, the Story of Sir Andreas de Harcla, Adrian Rogan (£8.95, ISBN 0 9523282 8 3)

A Riot of Thorn & Leaf, Dulcie Matthews (£7.95, ISBN 0 9540711 0 7)

Military Mountaineering, A History of Services Expeditions, 1945-2000, Retd. SAS Major Bronco Lane (Hardback, £25.95, ISBN 0952328216/Paperback, £17.95, ISBN 0952328267)

2041 - The Voyage South, Robert Swan (£8.95, 0 9523282 7 5)

Riding the Stang, Dawn Robertson (£9.99, ISBN 0 9523282 2 4)

Secrets and Legends of Old Westmorland, Peter Koronka & Dawn Robertson (Hardback, £17.95, ISBN 0 95232824 0) (Paperback, £11.95, ISBN 0 9523282 9 1)

The Irish Influence, Migrant Workers in Northern England, Harold Slight (£4.95, 0 9523282 5 9)

Soldiers and Sherpas, A Taste for Adventure, Brummie Stokes. (£19.95, 0 9541551 0 6)

North Country Tapestry, Sylvia Mary McCosh (£10, 0 9518690 0 0)

Between Two Gardens, The Diary of two Border Gardens, Sylvia Mary McCosh (£5.95, 0 9008111 7 X)

Dacre Castle, A short history of the Castle and the Dacre Family, E. H. A. Stretton (£5.50, 0 9518690 1 9)

Little Ireland, Memories of a Cleator Moor Childhood, Sean Close (£7.95, ISBN 095 4067 304)

A Slip from Grace, More tales from Little Ireland, Sean Close (£10.00, ISBN 095 4067 312)

You can order any of our books by writing to:
Hayloft Publishing Ltd., South Stainmore, Kirkby Stephen, Cumbria, CA17 4EU, UK.
Please enclose a cheque plus £2 for UK postage and packing.
or telephone: +44 (0)17683) 42300
For more information see: www.hayloft.org.uk